PRAISE FOR RAMONA KOVAL

'Ramona Koval has carved a reputation as a consummate book critic and interviewer. Her passion for storytelling and sharp analysis is turned inwards in *Bloodhound: Searching for My Father*, in which she asks herself: what is my life story? Her accessibly written forays into the science of DNA and familial lineages, and what makes us who we are, are beautifully intertwined with her meditations on identity and belonging...[*Bloodhound* is] an important reminder that history should never be forgotten.'

Books+Publishing

'She's a shining presence in the world of literature, here in Australia and right across the globe...Her voice is always recognisable, invigorating, familiar to us and greatly loved.'

Helen Garner

'*By the Book* takes us on intriguing journeys...The excitement with which Koval still approaches each new book, plunging in "head first, heart deep", furnishes the last words of this urbane and enlightening work of her own.'

Peter Pierce, *Weekend Australian*

'Irresistible...The voice [in *By the Book*] is easily recognisable as the one we know from her decades in radio: generous, warm and fearless.'

Kerryn Goldsworthy, *Australian Book Review*

'*By the Book* is a reminder of the role books can play in our lives. If you celebrate their contribution and appreciate their influence and artistry, then this is a story you will want to treasure.'

Weekly Review

Ramona Koval is a Melbourne writer, journalist, broadcaster and editor. She is an honorary fellow in the Centre for Advancing Journalism at the University of Melbourne. From 2006 to 2011 she presented Radio National's *Book Show*, and she has written for the *Age* and *Australian*. She is the author of *By the Book: A Reader's Guide to Life*.

ramonakoval.com

@ramonakoval

Bloodhound

RAMONA KOVAL

searching for my father

TEXT PUBLISHING
MELBOURNE AUSTRALIA

textpublishing.com.au

The Text Publishing Company
Swann House
22 William Street
Melbourne Victoria 3000
Australia

First published in 2015 by The Text Publishing Company

Book design by W. H. Chong
All photographs courtesy of the author
Typeset in Golden Cockerel ITC by J & M Typesetting
Printed in Australia by Griffin Press

National Library of Australia Cataloguing-in-Publication entry

Creator: Koval, Ramona, 1954– author.

Title: Bloodhound : searching for my father / by Ramona Koval.

ISBN: 9781922182760 (paperback)

ISBN: 9781925095685 (ebook)

Subjects: Koval, Ramona, 1954—Family. Holocaust survivors' families—Australia. Father and child.

Dewey Number: 929.20994

 This book is printed on paper certified against the Forest Stewardship Council® Standards. Griffin Press holds FSC chain-of-custody certification SGS-COC-005088. FSC promotes environmentally responsible, socially beneficial and economically viable management of the world's forests.

  This project has been assisted by the Commonwealth Government through the Australia Council, its arts funding and advisory body.

For my grandchildren,
and their children,
for ten generations

Contents

And will the dead person have exercised his right to carry a secret to his grave? After all, is that not one of the great rights of life, to know that we know something that we will never reveal to anyone?

CARLOS FUENTES

Oif a meisseh fregt men kain kasheh nit.
Don't ask questions about fairytales.

YIDDISH PROVERB

For in much wisdom is much grief:
and he that increaseth knowledge, increaseth sorrow.

ECCLESIASTES 1:18

1

Who wants to know?

DAD'S eightieth-birthday party was held late last century in his favourite restaurant, a cavernous space in a middle-class Melbourne suburb, with a tiled floor for easy cleaning, possibly even hosing down, and little in the way of warmth, charm or decoration. Clearly, you were here to eat until you were full.

Waiters balanced huge platters of food on their shoulders—grilled meats and fish and salads and dips and bread, bread, bread—delivering them to long tables of grandparents and their grandchildren, their daughters and sons-in-law, sons and daughters-in-law, and second and third cousins and their partners. The place forbade people from bringing their own drinks—instead you got them at the bar, or had them delivered to the table after a lengthy delay—and each time the waiters ventured down the aisles they were accosted by ten burly customers, hands grabbing their shirts and threatening to unbalance the heaped trays. *My water! Where's my Diet Coke? I asked for a cappuccino! It's been ten minutes already and I'm dying of thirst!*

Dad, on this, his day, had smuggled in orange juice and mineral water in a string bag. He'd stashed the bottles under his chair, from where he sneaked them out in full view of his grandchildren, his dark-brown eyes winking loudly: for if there can be such a thing as a winking noise, Dad had it in his repertoire. He was playing the big man, as my mother might have put it, a big shot with a string bag—as if this would fool anybody.

My mother's voice was in my ear, but not because she was sitting beside me. Her voice lived in my head. She had been dead for twenty-one years. She didn't make it to her fiftieth birthday, much less her eightieth. Each time Dad reached a new milestone I did the calculation. Why couldn't it be she who was celebrating, and he who was lying dead in the ground?

I know you're not supposed to wish people dead. Was it his fault that he had a new wife and a new life? They had been together for at least twenty-two years—another calculation I would do, justifying my outrage on Mama's behalf. I have always been good at calculations.

Mama had found a photograph of a strange woman along with a small hand mirror. They had been secured by a rubber band to the underside of the sun visor on the passenger side of our family car, a white 1963 Ford Falcon that Mama and Dad were still driving in the mid-1970s. The woman was standing by a dark-green shrub, smiling at the photographer, who may have been Dad.

She was attractive, I remember thinking, much too attractive for him, surely, a short man with greying black hair slicked straight back from his forehead. The girlfriend, as we came to think of her, was several years older but more vital-looking than Mama, who'd had chronic myeloid leukaemia for a couple of years by then.

Mama tucked the photo back under the sun visor and I don't remember it being mentioned again, although she and Dad could have argued about it in Polish and I wouldn't have known. They had a long history of fighting but also of mind games. In our family album of often out-of-focus Box Brownie black-and-white photos (all of which seemed to have been taken a long way away from the subjects, so it was hard to see who they were and what they were doing) there were two photos of Dad with another man and two women, strangers to me, on a jaunt in an open-top sports car. I'd never seen a car like that—I had no idea what they were doing together and who took the photo, why they were in the album and why Mama left them there.

He must have known she'd find the photo behind the sun visor. It was her car, too, and surely the rubber band in her eye line was a dead giveaway. Just as he must have known that everyone at the eightieth-birthday lunch would see his contraband drinks. He must have wanted them to.

Dad left Mama to set up house with the girlfriend, who later became his new wife, in January of the year of Mama's October death. It sounds bad. But most family stories are complicated.

My oldest nephew, then eleven, was sitting next to me at the birthday lunch. He was almost old enough to start preparing for his bar mitzvah, nearly a man, so he was allowed to taste the wine. I was teaching him to sip it slowly, to savour it. Not that I was an expert wine drinker. I don't really like its taste, preferring a shot of vodka. I agree with Ogden Nash that liquor is quicker.

Seeing this, his grandfather—and after all, this was Dad's day, and why, he must have thought, shouldn't he be the centre of attention—called out, 'Hey, sonny, watch this!' and downed a full glass of wine in three big gulps, then filled the glass to the top once more. I felt anger rise inside me as I watched him abrogate his grandfatherly duty to be wise and careful with the boy; to respect the wishes of his mother, my younger sister; and to support my gentle modelling of responsible drinking. (These views on grandfatherly behaviour came from television and films, as I never met my grandparents.) How, I thought, and not for the first time, could the old man possibly be related to me?

Indeed, as I cast my eyes up and down the table, I observed, again not for the first time, that there seemed to be a meeting of two tribes here. There was the straight-haired, redheaded tribe—my sister, her husband and two of their three children—and there was the taller, curly haired and blue-eyed tribe, my two daughters and me.

Any observer would have to say—and they have, over the years—that there was little physical evidence to link these people, except that they were all at this table, everyone except Dad fearing overeating and subsequent bloatedness, here to celebrate (while swearing under their breath to get this over and done with as quickly as possible) the eightieth birthday of this man, this short Jewish tailor from Poland, this survivor who was sent to the Treblinka death camp—twice, mind you, but that's another story—and who spent nearly two years hiding in a 'hole in the ground' with the Goldman brothers.

When I heard that phrase I thought of Dad as an animal, a rat or a fox, living in a burrow. How did you do that? Later I understood that they hid in a small cellar under the kitchen floor of a rural shack. But the image of him as a hunted thing, a night scavenger, stayed with me.

He was worried then, he once told me, that if he survived the war he would be an alcoholic after drinking daily the bootleg vodka they made from potato peelings, in part payment to the peasant who allowed them to hide there, despite the threat to his own life. How they manufactured the drink I never asked, and neither would you if you'd met the man, but there it was, his worry, and he'd tell us that the others taunted him for not wanting to drink, saying that teetotallers would wake up in the morning and know that was the best they were going to feel all day.

For a while I thought Dad's story of the hole in the ground and drinking and hangovers and feeling better later in the day was original. But I heard Dean Martin tell the same joke on TV in the 1960s, and I understood that Dad would've had no problem with lifting the joke and putting it there in the same hole he was occupying, with no regard for time and place and history. For him, jokes were more important than mere history: they were his lingua franca.

It was my regard for time and place and history that set me off on a journey which had begun with the ambiguity and secrecy surrounding my dear dead Mama. In fact, for as long as I can remember I had wondered how I could be related to Dad.

My Real Father, I figured, must have been someone who Mama loved, but for some reason he was unable to live with us. That is why we had Dad. Mama was a mysterious woman whose own survival story, of which I knew scant details, involved her assuming a false identity and narrowly avoiding death, thanks to her fine acting skills. It was never easy to ask her something directly and get a clear answer. She outwitted Hitler's plans for her, so how could I hope to carry out a successful interrogation? Anyway, as you know, she died two decades before Dad's eightieth-birthday party and the chain of events it set in motion.

Ten years before the birthday lunch, Mama's close friend Bernadette had called me at work. It was a surprise to hear from her, as the last time we'd spoken was a week after Mama's death. I'd asked her then if she could tell me anything about Mama's life and my conception. I knew in my bones that things were not straightforward, and now that Mama was no longer around to moderate my inquisitive-ness I thought I could raise the topic with her best friend. But Bern was not for turning: if my mother had wanted me to know something, she would have told me herself. And if Mama had told her a secret, Bern couldn't possibly tell me.

I was twenty-three, a mother with a two-year-old child and pregnant with my second, and she was forty-three. I had no way of arguing with her and, besides, what did I know of the complexities of their friendship and sworn secrets?

After that conversation, Bern disappeared from my life. I imagine she thought that I might be too curious and too persuasive and not willing to let things lie, including my dead Mama's wishes. She might well have been right.

And then, out of the blue, a decade after Mama's death, Bern was on the phone telling me that a man had asked after me at a house auction in a suburb near where I lived, asking Bern if I was married and if I had children and what kind of work I did. He wanted to know if I was happy.

The man was a stranger to me, but not to her. Bern said that if I still had any interest in finding out the circumstances of my birth, I might like to start with him. She gave me his last name, Dunne, and told me that he was one of two brothers who used to own a clothing factory in which Mama worked as a finisher, sewing on buttons and embroidering collars, before I was born.

Why would a stranger want to know if I was happy? If I had children? Dad had never asked if I was happy.

I looked up the name in the phone book and rang the number for a home near where the auction was held, but there was no answer. I tried to imagine the conversation that might ensue. *Hello? I was wondering if you're the man who was recently at an auction and asked a woman named Bernadette if I was married and had children and was happy—and if you are that man, are you also my Real Father?* You need a certain inner strength or a well-honed sense of the absurd to go through with something like that, neither of which I was blessed with at the time. I didn't call again.

What was it about Dad's eightieth birthday, then, that spurred me to follow up on the clue, many years after the opportunity first presented itself? The possibility that this might be his last birthday, and that I could finally investigate my suspicions without hurting him? That would be a noble answer.

In truth, I was so angry with Dad for guzzling the wine—the way he undermined my careful instruction of his grandson, the way he wanted to upstage the boy, the infantile and disrespectful display of wilfulness at the table—that I left the restaurant with an overwhelming urge to make the connection long severed. I telephoned Bern that afternoon.

I asked her to repeat the story of the man at the auction. And when she did, more or less word for word, I said that I thought Mama had been wrong. She had gone to her grave with a secret that wasn't hers to keep. I had spent some years and much money on the psychoanalyst's couch, trying to understand my estrangement from Dad. I was now in my forties, a few years younger than Mama was when she died at forty-nine. It was time to make some sense of all this.

Bern told me that she had first met the man Dunne when Mama took her to buy men's suits at wholesale prices from the shop at the factory where Mama had worked for two brothers in the early 1950s.

'The older brother was shorter, and he was terribly kind to your mother,' Bern said. 'The younger one glared at her, and never spoke. But I could feel the tension between them. He ate her up with his eyes. I knew that there had been something between them, but your mother never said.'

I liked the idea of the man eating my mother up with his eyes. She was a lovely woman, though not emotionally open, and she was terribly unhappy with Dad. They fought constantly, and I cannot remember a single act of affection between them. Never a kiss, never a warm touch.

Bern's story of the younger brother immediately assumed great significance. Why did he glare at Mama—why didn't they speak? And why did she take her friend to the factory, anyway: was she hoping to irritate or inflame him? Or just to get Bern a bargain suit?

I see Mama preparing for the venture, making sure her stockings are straight, applying lipstick, spraying Amour Amour by Jean Patou behind her ears, between her breasts and on each wrist. She holds her head high, but who knows what goes on in her mind on the way to the factory? Once there, she doesn't speak to the man, her eyes haughty, looking straight through him, not looking down, no eyelid batting. No batting whatsoever.

I've tried to buy Amour Amour in all the airports I've passed through, even in Paris, but it's no longer produced. I once bought a stash from a website offering rare fragrances, but when it arrived I could smell a bad counterfeit. Jean Patou invented Joy, 'the costliest perfume in the world', in 1925. His Amour Amour, 'a floral scent for brunettes', was released in the same year. How did Mama get hold of her first bottle? I can only afford to buy perfume duty free: how could a poor factory worker develop such expensive taste?

Until the second conversation with Bern I'd never thought about it. A child accepts that this is how things are and that they are like this in all families, until she finds out otherwise.

Mama and Dad didn't share a bedroom. I assumed this was normal until one of their survivor friends noticed that our master bedroom contained two single beds. 'How can you do anything in a single bed?' he shouted at the assembled guests, including us kids. I was puzzled. What did you need to do in a bed but sleep? Then he saw me getting a toy or a book from the room, and he understood that the beds were for my mother and me. He exploded with derision. Single beds were bad enough, but separate rooms—that was pathological.

Having gleaned what I could from Bern, I scoured the telephone directory. There were several Dunnes, a name that was strangely non-European and unlike those of Mama and Dad's friends. At first I assumed it had been anglicised, as happened to some who arrived here bearing Polish or Russian or Hungarian names with unfamiliar letters and combinations of consonants that troubled the local authorities. Then it dawned on me that he could have been an Englishman. *Fee-fi-fo-fum, I smell the blood of an Englishman.*

My sister and I had been brought up as the daughters of Polish Jews. This meant cabbage rolls and poppy-seed cake, bargaining and Yiddish melodies. Now I was toying with the idea that I was half English. *Mad dogs and Englishmen go out in the midday sun.* Being English meant being tight-lipped (my ungenerous interpretation of stiff-upper-lippedness), drabness (was this impression just from films like *Mrs. Miniver*, set during the London Blitz?), and using only one egg to make a cake. I always used at least eight. I scoured my character for latent Englishness.

But of course! My middle name is Alice: an utterly English name. How did Mama, who called me Ramona on my birth certificate (so that, come the next oppressive time, people wouldn't assume I was Jewish) and Rivkele at home, come up with my second name? I dismissed the evidence: that my Spanish first name had come about through my mother looking for something non-Jewish starting with 'R', and had heard the popular song 'Ramona' on the radio.

I imagined a less prosaic reason for my second name, perhaps that Mr Dunne's mother was called Alice and I was named for her. This was the secret sign between them that I was his daughter. My heart pounded—already, it seemed, the pieces of the puzzle were falling into place.

I tried to think of good Englishness. Garden beds and hollyhocks and cream teas and Jane Austen. I had tried to like Austen, and I was a fan of irony, but I was completely uninterested in marrying well and the affairs of the landed gentry in the southern counties of Regency England. But that was when I wasn't English. Maybe now I could admit Jane Austen into my being.

I rang the number for the Dunne in the suburb near the auction all those years before, and a middle-aged man answered the phone. I asked him if he was related to the brothers who'd owned a clothing factory in the 1950s and he said: 'Who wants to know?' He sounded like a character from *The Sopranos*, but without the New Jersey accent.

I explained that my mother used to work for the Dunne brothers, and I was researching her life and hoping to speak to anyone who might be able to tell me something about the time when she worked at the factory. The man told me that his father was living with him, but he was now deaf and not so good at seeing either. I took a breath and asked if his father was the older or the younger brother.

The older one. Joseph. The younger one had died some years before. Max Dunne—in the original Polish, Majlech Adunaj. Melech in Hebrew, meaning 'king'. He used to eat my mother up with his eyes. Now those eyes were closed forever.

If Max was my father, I was certainly not half English. But was he my father? I'm not sure why I decided to tell the whole story to a stranger on the phone, but I did. He must have sounded open. And to his credit, he didn't hang up. He was intrigued partly because he recognised my name from my newspaper articles and radio shows, he said; and partly, as I was shortly to learn, because he hated his uncle Max. Perhaps he hoped to hear something scandalous about him. For his uncle had been a married man, and had a son who, we established, was four years old when I was born.

'What does he look like?' I ventured.

'Blond, blue eyes, curly hair.'

'And what do you look like?'

'Like Paul Newman, only better-looking. But there is something you should know about my uncle. He spent years as a slave labourer in Auschwitz, and he was made into a beast. He was a twisted, difficult man who was cruel to his family and to my father. His son had to run away from him. The war ruined him. Maybe it's best you never met him.'

He offered to mail me a photograph of his uncle, and rang off.

2

A shame and a disgrace

I'M asking you to imagine her as I remember her, but not in those last months as she seemed to shrink before me, her hair thinning, her body disappearing, the breasts I used to rest my head against reversing to flatness like a time-lapse film played backwards. In those last months she was light enough for me to carry to the bathroom and back, and soon getting in and out of the bath was too much for her, and I washed her frail body in bed.

No, I'm thinking of her a few years before that, getting ready for an evening at the theatre with Bern, a beautiful woman, a former model who we once saw in a television commercial for toilet paper. Toilet *tissue*, it was called. Clothes always looked great on Bern, and she was taller and slimmer than Mama, but as far as I knew she was a Catholic virgin when she married and she didn't seem entirely comfortable in the body she'd been blessed with. Mama had a different quality, which I now recognise as sex appeal. Before she fell ill, she said that if I had breasts as good as hers when I got to her age, I'd be very lucky. She had seen a lot, and she probably radiated a woman-of-the-world ambience.

It was hard for me to pick up on it then, as a teenage daughter called in to zip up the back of her dress.

Amour Amour wafted from her neck as usual, and I could see the small depression in the skin of her upper back, just over the shoulder blade. She once told me it was a bullet hole from the time she was arrested by the Gestapo. If I had the chance now, I would ask her to elaborate. Back then, I was horrified. I knew that the mothers of other kids at school probably didn't have bullet wounds in their backs. I was forever trying to smooth over the differences between their white-bread families and my dark-rye one, so I avoided difficult subjects.

Why, I would wonder, did I find it so hard to ask Mama the questions that came to me again and again? Why did she have this force field around her?

I knew little about her life before me. I did know she was from a deeply religious Orthodox family where the men prayed and worked the fields, and the women in their wigs ran the bakery. For generations the family had lived and farmed in Wyrozęby, a tiny hamlet in eastern Poland. Her parents had been childhood sweethearts, if such a thing was possible, and both sets of grandparents were next-door neighbours in the village. Her father died when she was two months old—he'd developed a fatal case of pneumonia after swimming across an almost frozen river to be home for her birth—and she was brought up in her extended family.

After the Germans invaded Poland, the family was transported to the ghetto in Sokołów Podlaski, a town a short distance from Wyrozęby. By the summer of 1942 there were rumours about deportations of Jews from the nearby

Siedlce ghetto and from Warsaw—they would be killed at Treblinka. Jews from Sokołów Podlaski had been sent to an unknown destination from which nobody had returned.

Mama was the only one of the family in the Sokołów Podlaski ghetto who was fair and blue-eyed (she took after her father's people rather than her mother's, with their darker and more Semitic looks), so she was chosen as the one most likely to escape using false Aryan identity papers. Aged fourteen, she said goodbye to her mother and brother and other relatives, walked the ninety-odd kilometres to Warsaw, and disappeared into the city.

She became Alina Kołakowska: Catholic, Warsaw-born, twenty-one. She plaited her hair to straighten its natural waves and pinned the plaits to the top of her head, a traditional Polish hairstyle. Mama was Alina for two and half years, revealing her true identity to no one. This little I gleaned of her life during the war.

And Dad? Here in Melbourne, he was a cutter in a factory which, by the time I was aware of such things, was mass producing cheap T-shirts and shorts and skivvies for Target. It was many steps down from making men's suits and women's 'costumes', which he was trained to do before the war, and which he continued to do after it in Paris, then in Melbourne after their arrival in 1949.

Dad liked his bosses and the people in the factory who responded to his jokes and stories. He wasn't deep. Not like her. It was hard to imagine them together.

Each year their survivor friends would gather for a fancy-dress party to dance and celebrate their lives. One of the circle made home movies and from one party there's a fleeting, trembling sequence showing the guests walking up a stairwell towards the camera. Mama arrives in a white kaftan with bell sleeves which she'd made that day from an old bed sheet. It had a matching trim on the collar, sleeves and the headband. She is wearing a faux-copper peace sign she borrowed from me, so it must be 1970. Her hair is shoulder-length and oddly honey-coloured, and she disconcerts by folding her arms in front as if she were a Native American woman. She smiles faintly and her eyes give nothing away.

Dad ascends the stairs at least twenty seconds after her arrival, possibly more, as I'm not sure how much time was removed in the editing. He looks like a cross between a Mafiosi hoodlum and a plump Roy Orbison, in an open-necked black-and-white checked shirt, with dark glasses, a silver chain hanging over his belly and his straight dark hair brushed forwards. He holds a cigarette between his fingers and scowls. Maybe he was looking for her, or just needed a drink. They couldn't even arrive together.

He liked to be the life of the party and on the surface he was all bluster. It was a shallow crust, though, and you couldn't ask him questions about his past unless you were prepared to deal with his sobbing. I soon learned not to open the floodgates. Possibly I saved up all the questions for later, for my years as a journalist, a professional asker of questions.

In the 1960s reparation pensions became available to Holocaust survivors. We'd get letters from Germany via a firm of Melbourne solicitors, Kahn Clahr & Garsa, that dealt with survivors' claims. The gothic script and long dark-cream envelopes made it seem as if the missives came directly from the Third Reich.

Each year Mama and Dad had to attend the German consulate in Melbourne to prove they were still alive. This was traumatic for both of them. They went separately. Mama came back from one of these visits and said she'd told the consular officer that Hitler hadn't succeeded in killing her yet. It must have been traumatic for the younger officers, too: I don't imagine Mama was the only survivor who took the need for proof of life so personally.

For their initial assessments my parents had to submit to psychiatric evaluations to determine the extent of their damage. Mama showed me the psychiatric report of Dad's mental state. The lawyers were claiming that he had ninety per cent incapacitation. Ninety per cent, she repeated. I thought that meant Dad was ninety per cent insane—a humiliation I hoped to keep hidden from my friends. The report described his memories of and dreams about cleaning up the square in his hometown of Siedlce after German soldiers had mown down groups of his school friends and neighbours. He had to pick up the brains of the dead with his hands. I imagined them dripping through his fingers. When I looked at his hands, in my mind's eye I could see the blood. He seemed tainted and disgusting.

'Now you might understand why your father is the way he is,' Mama said. She didn't show me her evaluation, and I didn't ask to see it. One report like that was enough for any girl. It was already one too many.

And now, a few decades later, I was about to cloud the mix with the twisted and cruel (according to his nephew) Max Dunne. A photograph of the man who might have been my real father was en route, yet my willingness to believe was wavering. The father I had was infuriating and inadequate, but I remembered that he had given me my first typewriter, an old Olivetti portable that someone offered him; he had taught me to drive; and at least he hadn't been made into a beast in Auschwitz. I thought about being the daughter of a cruel and twisted man. I thought about my mother lying down with that man.

And I remembered her picking me up at the end of one of my shifts at a knitting factory in Collingwood. I worked there over the summer after my fourteenth birthday, fixing the labels onto acrylic jumpers and cardigans. It was 1968 and psychedelics were all the rage: hot pink and purple, lime green and navy blue, orange and brown in swirly geometric patterns.

Mama took me to a room off the large open factory floor: windowless and concrete-walled, with a naked globe hanging down, like an interrogation room in a spy film. There was a low metal bed with a small pillow and a rough grey blanket. She asked me what I thought went on in here, and I said that it must be the sick bay, like at school, and this was where you could rest if you had a headache or period pain.

Mama laughed scornfully. This, she said, was where the owner of the factory took any girl he summoned from the floor if he wanted to have sex with her. And she had to go, or she'd lose her job. If I was having thoughts about leaving school and working in a factory, she wanted me to understand that this was what I would face.

I was baffled. I was an excellent student; I loved going to school; and I had no intention of leaving behind my beloved maths and science, English and French for a job in the rag trade. What was she talking about?

Now I could think about this encounter in a new light. Was she showing me what happened in the factory when she worked for the Beast of Auschwitz? Was I the result of a tawdry transaction at work—was that the reason she couldn't bring herself to tell me? But what kind of secret-keeping made her introduce me to such an unexpected, ugly scenario: was it subconscious?

At the time I filed the episode away with Mama's other mysterious lessons on life. Like being careful not to fall asleep in the snow, no matter how tired and hungry you were, because you could freeze to death. I hadn't even seen snow, but I remembered the lesson, just in case.

And when it came, the envelope, the holder of all this mystery, the clue to an answer for my many questions, was small and unprepossessing.

Just before I opened it, I sat in the bay window of my sitting room, looking out into the garden. I loved the comfortable yellow couch, which I had bought with the money I earned from writing, and I liked to read there, stretched out on my own words, as I imagined it. I knew that I had to use all of my critical faculties—my training as a scientist and my experience as a journalist—to evaluate whatever evidence was before me, despite what I wanted to find.

I was looking for evidence that supported my deeply held conviction about a hidden story. I thought that searching the faces of strangers for hints of a connection seemed pathetic. And here I was, about to do it.

In my hands was a photograph taken in 1937 of a twenty-four-year-old man, before he embarked on his journey to the inferno. The man looked familiar, and I wondered if I had seen him before. He was handsome and taller than the people next to him, who'd been cut out of this photo except for their shoulders. And there was something especially familiar about the eyes, their depth, their set, and the shape of the face.

A thought, alarming yet moving, came to me. It was *my* face. This is what I might have looked like, had I been a man of twenty-four in 1937. I drove with the photograph on the seat beside me to several friends, and asked them to tell me what they saw. 'The eyes,' they said, 'and the shape of the face.' I carried the photograph with me, and tested it with workmates and with strangers. They all agreed.

I called Max's nephew and told him that everyone said the man in the picture looked like me.

'Well then,' he said, 'you'd better come over and meet us. But don't tell my father that you think we're related. He's nearly ninety, and for him it would be a shame and a disgrace.' *A shandeh un a charpeh* is the way you say it in Yiddish.

This I agreed to do, but I felt resistance. Why should I be ashamed of the possible story of my birth? It was hardly my decision to have my parents go outside the bonds of holy matrimony. Was I the sort of person a man might be ashamed of having as a relative? Still, I held back my feelings, because I was on a roll and I was following a trail, and made an appointment for four o'clock the next day.

It was a Friday in summer when the temperature was over forty degrees, and there I was, in a summer frock and clutching a large wooden-framed photograph of Mama with me at age three on her knee, ostensibly so that the old man could look at it and might even recognise the woman who worked for him forty-five years before, and shopped at his wholesale showroom later, and was the mother of his secret, shameful niece.

When his son opened the door, the first thing I saw was his wavy hair and blue eyes. In his late fifties, he was still a striking man. We shook hands and laughed at the absurdity of the situation, me clutching the photo frame, sworn not to mention that I had already seen a photo of his father's dead brother. Soon I was sitting at their kitchen table and, while the old man was charming and friendly, he didn't recognise Mama, although he said what an attractive woman she'd been.

I wondered why he couldn't place her. Did they have so many underlings in the days of vast numbers of women bent over Singer treadle machines, like those you see in old newsreels? How could the centre of my being, my Mama, mean so little to him?

After his son engineered it, the old man started to show me the family photo album, starting with shots of his grandchildren and his wife. All the while I was dying for him to get to those of his brother and his brother's son, my possible half-brother.

'And who's this?' I asked eventually.

'That's my brother Majlech, in our tailor's shop in the town of Mława in Poland before the war.' The same face that I had seen in that first photograph, smiling now, and here again with a family group. His eyes. They almost told you they had seen many things, even as you knew they were yet to see many more. Uninterested in Joseph's wife's side of the family, I was cavalier, desperate to get to my quarry. I was a bloodhound and the trail was hot. I drank black coffee and asked for another cup, stretching out the time I could have with the album, and eventually came across a photograph of his brother's son, who also looked like me.

And all of this only one week after I'd started my search. I was excited, and then I felt pathetic again, like a child trying to ingratiate herself into a family to whom she is really a stranger. Is that my father? Are they my uncles? Is this my grandmother? Was this man, this butcher named Adunaj in a provincial northern Polish town, my grandfather?

I thought of P. D. Eastman's story for children *Are You My Mother?* A chick hatches when his mother is away looking for food, and he starts searching for her in all the wrong places. He asks 'Are you my mother?' of a kitten, a hen, a dog and a cow, and then he turns to inanimate objects: a boat, a plane and finally a great power shovel on a building site. The story has a happy ending, when the shovel places the bird back in the nest as his mother returns with dinner. Would I find the power shovel of my dreams? Not that I was expecting dinner, as all the personnel were long dead.

I felt a pang of envy seeing all these photographs from Poland before the war. Joseph had emigrated in 1937 (under the names Izrael Yosck Adunaj and Israel Josek Adunaj, according to documents I later found in the National Archives), and must have brought many photos with him, or perhaps his family sent them in the ensuing couple of years.

Growing up, my sister and I had no set of photographs. There was one of Mama's grandfather, an old man with a black cap, a long coat and a long beard. She said the beard was red, like my sister's hair. There was a group photograph that included Mama's mother, who wore a large sun hat and whose face we couldn't really see. These must have been sent by distant cousins in Israel, and I knew they were a source of pain for her. To my shame I can't even find them now—I fear they were hidden at the back of a piece of furniture that I donated to charity when she died. I was never privy to her hiding places.

I might have envied these people their family album, but at least I discovered that Adunaj was a Polish name meaning 'from the Danube'. From the Danube to Adunaj to Dunne. I was relieved again not to have to think of myself as English.

The old man was getting tired. He became puzzled and asked me to explain again why I was there. It was time for me to go.

His son gave me the name of the daughter of Max and his wife's best friends. He thought she might be able to give me more information about what kind of person Max had been. He didn't know exactly what had happened to Max in Auschwitz or even how long he'd been there.

If Max had had some close friends for many years, it was possible he wasn't so terrible. He must have had some social skills. I was happy to doubt the Beast of Auschwitz story.

And the half-brother, Max's son: his name was Alan, he lived in Queensland and he was close to his mother. Contacting him now might upset Max's widow, and could lead back to Dad. I'd decided that surviving the Holocaust was one thing for Dad, but surviving a challenge to his fatherhood was quite another. I didn't want to risk it.

It was still over forty degrees outside, with a cloudless sky. The kind of day you remember from school years, trudging home, when the sun made you squint so you couldn't see the road ahead and you could hardly breathe.

3

Something to find, something to see

BEFORE Dad's eightieth birthday and the call to Bern, before I sat with the two men at their kitchen table poring over their family album, I was invited to attend a writers' workshop in Prague and conduct interviews there. When I'd looked at a map of the world to work out my route, I'd realised that Poland was just north of the Czech Republic. I'd never looked closely at this part of the globe before. My parents had never pulled out a map to show me where they grew up. The idea came to me that, if I was going as far as Prague, I may as well go to Warsaw, too. And if I was going to Warsaw, I may as well visit the towns where Mama and Dad were born. I had no idea of where these towns were in relation to one another and to the capital.

I took my recording equipment with me and made a radio documentary that I called *The Cellar, the Hinges and the Copper Samovar*. I liked the title. It reminded me of folk tales, which often list things in threes. And I liked the absurdity of the premise. It was about the search for three things that seemed impossible to find: the cellar, the 'hole in the ground' where Dad hid with the two Goldman brothers; some iron hinges—the work of my children's paternal great-great-grandfather, a blacksmith who, like other boys, had his thumbs removed to avoid the draft for Tsar Nicholas II's Russian army, as you couldn't fire a musket without thumbs—which were on the windows and doors of a house in a small village beside the Bug River; and the house where my maternal great-grandfather, a baker, had sat by his window drinking forty cups of tea a day from the copper samovar.

Looking for the cellar where Dad had hidden, I was armed with only his hand-drawn map of Siedlce, which lies around ninety kilometres east of Warsaw. When I'd invited him to accompany me, in an effort to improve the connection between us, he had declined.

On the recording I made at the time, he says:

It's very hard for me to discourage you, because you are a young person. And I don't want to be the one to discourage you from something, because the human nature is always...it wants something to find, it wants something to see; you think you'll see something, you'll learn something. That, I don't want to say. But me as a person, I don't see the reason for it, to go to Poland.

For me to come back, that is the worst thing what can happen to me. There is not a cemetery there...Like I said, I don't think even the grave of my brother is still there, I don't believe in that; I believe it's all demolished, it's all broken down. After fifty years nobody's there, not a soul.

If I go in the street where it was the ghetto then I'll see the street, I'll remember the blood was flowing there. How can I go, how can I look at that? But you are young, you are looking for opportunities, you are looking for wisdom, you think maybe...If you want to go, I can't tell you not to go—I leave it to your judgements. But I, you will never persuade me to go. To me, Poland is a Jewish huge cemetery.

On my first night in Warsaw, while I was eating at a table outside the Hotel Europejski opposite the Saxon Gardens, the strains of familiar music wafted from the dining room. I could hardly believe I was hearing 'If I Were a Rich Man' from *Fiddler on the Roof,* the kitsch American adaptation of 'Tevye the Milkman' and other short stories of the Yiddish writer Sholem Aleichem. The trio played each phrase enthusiastically, the violin making virtuoso features of the klezmer lilts. Here, in a country almost without Jews, the diners hummed along with Jewish melodies.

This was my first experience of being a living Polish folk memory. Most Jews had been killed during the war or had left soon afterwards when pogroms began to eliminate the few survivors. Poland had been a home for Jews for hundreds of years, and now some Poles seemed quite sentimental about the culture that had thrived here. In several towns I found tours that offered experiences of the Jewish past. I felt disoriented: authentic and yet out of place.

I'd engaged a guide and translator, a university mathematician who could make more money taking people around Poland investigating their roots. His father had been Jewish and his mother not, and he'd made a study of the history of Polish Jewry. From Warsaw we drove east in his battered blue Skoda to the town where Dad was born, to Siedlce—*Si-ed-letz-e* in Polish and Shedletz in Yiddish.

Dad had hidden in the cellar of a cottage outside town that was owned by a Polish family with a small farmstead. He'd reached this haven after making a narrow escape from the Treblinka death camp.

According to Dad, people were told that the Siedlce ghetto was overcrowded and that those in charge were worried about typhoid spreading, and hence they were being sent to a 'better camp'. Dad's mother and sisters and their families were sent to Treblinka. The people in the ghetto knew nothing, but they were suspicious. After three days Dad could not stand being without his family any longer, so he joined the old and infirm on the trains leaving for Treblinka, to look for his mother. As they arrived, he saw columns of naked people standing, waiting to go into 'barracks' for showers and leaving bundles of clothing on the ground.

As he was moving with the others, a man also in his mid-twenties came up to him. 'Don't go with that line,' he whispered. 'Tell me, what are you doing here?' Dad said he'd come to look for his mother and family, who'd arrived three days before. 'Don't look for them—they have gone to the gas chambers. Their bodies are already up the crematorium chimney. If you want to save yourself, come and help me.'

Dad helped him pick up all the clothing on the ground. They carried the bundles to the empty, dirty cattle wagons and stacked them high. The man told Dad to hide with him beneath a stack. They watched and waited, and eventually the door was closed and they heard a whistle outside the carriage. The train moved slowly out of Treblinka.

More than fifty years later, as the car pulled in to Siedlce, I saw some graffiti on a wall. It was a drawing of a Star of David in a hangman's noose. My translator told me the writing next to it said: *A good Jew is a dead Jew.* I was alarmed and amazed, but he was at pains to explain: 'Quite often, you know, the children are writing this and they really don't understand what they are writing. Probably they didn't see a Jew in their life.'

We were there to find an empty hole in the ground at an unknown address some distance out of town. At least I knew roughly the direction. It was a romantic and impossible task. The translator was happy enough to indulge me, and I was amusing myself with the mission.

Before I left for Poland I'd studied the map that Dad had drawn. I'd asked him to indicate the location of his hiding place, but the only thing on the page was a smudged pencilled arrow at the left edge, pointing off the page. It was absurd. It was perfect for my absurd quest.

He was terribly nervy that day, having drawn me the map but not wanting me to use it. On the recording he says:

Here is Warsaw, it was two hours' drive to Warsaw, but I went out of Siedlce, but it could be maybe one kilometre or maybe one and a half kilometres. And I'll write you down here, a map, look what I write you down here...This is the station, the railway station, you

come down the main street, I've forgotten the name
of this street...the street from the station to town.

When I arrived in Siedlce the map was all but useless, of
course. I had another one I'd picked up in the foyer of the
cheap hotel where I was staying. Dad had told me he lived
in Szkoła Ulica—School Street—at number 13. He'd remembered there was an electricity substation on the corner of
the street and, at the end of it, the Jewish cemetery. It wasn't
the best part of town. At first he told me that if he knew the
cemetery still existed he might join me, as his brother was
buried there, but then he demurred, saying he was sure
nothing existed there anymore.

In fact, the cemetery did still exist, but by the time I saw
it the graves were overgrown with weeds and many of the
headstones were smashed beyond recognition. It was used
as a shortcut across the paddocks. Dad's street was rundown, its wooden houses weather-greyed, paint peeling off
window frames and fences leaning, and there were some
vacant lots where houses had once stood. My translator
talked with a few locals and reported their suspicions that
I wanted to claim back land from them. Dad's family had
been renters, so there was no chance of that. Yet I didn't feel
like reassuring them.

A woman of advanced years, her red-dyed hair wild
and her eyes painted black with kohl, stopped us. She was
breathless, speaking at a great pace. The translator said:

She is a 'queen of songs' and she would like to go to
perform in Warsaw but unfortunately her whole

correspondence is stolen, so no letters are arriving
for her address because of the son of this older guy,
we were talking to him before, this is the worst guy
in the neighbourhood. Nevertheless she will go to
Warsaw and will try to make a comeback. Many
buildings in the street were in her possession, but
also were stolen from her by Jewish people. The
radio stations, the television stations and the Jewish
mafia is governing here, and all the power is derived
from her songs.

I wanted him to ask her how the Jews were running everything when there were no Jews here, but I saw that he'd rather
not. He didn't want to prolong the conversation, he said,
because she was crazy, a sick person. I asked if he thought
she was talking like that because she thought I was Jewish.
Probably not, he replied. It was just the kind of conversation
she might have any day, with anyone. 'Thirty per cent of
the people we've met today,' he said with a mathematician's
precision, 'have been either drunk or mad.'

Number 13 turned out to be a vacant block. As I stared
at it, I tried to visualise a house there, and in the house Dad,
the youngest of four children, and his widowed mother,
a sharecropper who cultivated and sold a portion of the
apples from an attached orchard—but the image didn't
come to me. I didn't feel connected to this block on this
street, with its suspicious neighbours and madwoman's
accusations. Though I didn't know it then, I had nothing to
do with this place save for a few stories.

Dad had spoken of his adored older brother, Herschel:

My brother came to the place I was working [as a labourer in a work camp] and he had some papers from his office at the petrol station allowing him to walk the streets freely, day or night. He came to the gate and showed the papers and they called me forward and let me go with my brother. I was still covered in black soot and he had arranged a shower for me, and he told me he had a place for me to hide. It was at a Polish man's house called Władek, together with another two brothers called Goldman. That same evening he went with me to the hiding place. It was two or three miles out of town in a cellar under the barn, with a trapdoor from the kitchen. He stayed with me one night, and the next day he went back, telling me he would return. He never did.

In the cellar by candlelight on all sorts of pieces of paper I started to write a diary of events from the first day of the war. I missed my family terribly, my mother, brother and sisters and their families. I cried day and night, and the pieces of paper were wet with my tears.

How they dig this hole, my brother, these two brothers—I wasn't there and I don't know how they digged it. What they did was a little house just with one room, a little bit back from the highway. In that room was two beds standing with the table, and a cooking oven which went on wood. So what they do—look, this is the oven [he scribbled a plan of the room in the hut]—and what they did, they dig the hole in front of the oven, just to jump down, and from the hole they dig a big place that you can lie down there with some wooden planks. So to go down to this hole we had to jump down and then we went there, hiding like rats,

sitting on these things. Then the wood trapdoor went
down, they put a mat on it, so when you walked in you
wouldn't find nothing...As soon as somebody went
out, they knocked, so we went out from the cellar, we
opened the trapdoor and we came out in the house.
You see, this is the hut which I survived. This, I must
give it to you. How can you recognise a hut like this?

Dad was showing me a photograph that I had never seen
before, taken in 1945 according to the pencil writing on the
back. It was of an older man sitting outside a house with his
wife and, standing behind them, their daughter. You could
see a line of the roof and a trellis. There was a name on the
back, too. 'Now I see his name was Władek Bimbrowski,'
Dad said. 'The writing says here: "He called me *son*."'

I asked Dad if he remembered anything about what
stood around the house, a marker, a shop, a fork in the road.

No, nothing. When you travel on the highway, the
south side of the town, you've got houses like this going
on all...Maybe one is a wood one, one has a few bricks,
the other one is made from timber, you see. But like
I said, every few hundred metres is a house, is a little
house. You wouldn't see a huge space empty because
there's houses one after another.

I wanted to find this Bimbrowski and thank him, or thank
whoever was left of his family, for sheltering Dad and
thereby ensuring my own safe passage into the world. But
at the Siedlce Registry Office, which my guide called the
Palace of Records, there was no trace of him. No luck either

in the Palace of Maps. I searched for birth and death certificates that might have survived the war, hoping to spot traces
of my roots in this community. I did find a man with the same
surname as Dad, who died in 1908 at the grand old age of one
hundred. He was called Gedalia and his profession was listed
as 'beggar'. He must have been a brilliant one to live so long.

I asked to see my parents' wedding certificate. For two
hours the archivists searched, without success. The last
thing they did was look through a book titled 'Unfiled
documents, those incomplete or without dates'. By this
stage it felt like another of my hopeless quests. I felt like the
queen of hopeless quests.

Then my translator called out. He couldn't believe it:
they had found something. There was Mama and Dad's
wedding certificate, with their signatures at the bottom of
the page, the handwriting I would recognise anywhere—
but no other parts of the certificate were filled in.

My translator explained, after speaking to the woman
in charge, that Mama and Dad had been in a hurry: 'So there
was this rabbi here and they said "I do", but there was no
time to make a proper certificate. They signed here and
didn't pick it up later for completion.'

Dad had told me that after hiding in the cellar he was
liberated at the end of 1944, when the Russians came to
town. He said he met the girl who would be his wife on the
streets of the town a few months later, and married her 'not
for love but for pity and loneliness'.

Mama and Dad were in such a rush because they had
to register their religious wedding to ensure that in the
future there would be no trouble getting passports to travel

together. A new birth certificate was made for Mama: they lied about her date of birth because she was underage. They didn't stay to pick up the document as it was the day after the Kielce pogrom, when forty-six Jewish concentration-camp survivors returning to their homes were murdered by their neighbours. Instead they escaped to Berlin by Russian army transport for the price of a bottle of vodka.

After I saw the abandoned marriage certificate in the Palace of Records, I drove several kilometres out of town in the direction of the arrow on Dad's map. There was no sign that this or that house or barn was the one I was looking for.

When I got back to the hotel, I recorded my call:

Hi Dad, guess who it is...Good...And guess where I'm ringing from? I'm in Siedlce. It's incredible. I'm good. Listen, we went to see Szkoła Ulica but there's no house there. No. So I found the Jewish cemetery. Yes. All the headstones are broken. No, it's all right, Dad, listen... Listen...Okay, Dad, I'm healthy...No, wait a minute, just calm down. I want to ask you a question. To find that place where you hid, we took...Hang on a second... Yes, okay, but there's a branch in the road. One road is called Terespolska and one street, Siedlecka, goes to the border of Belarus. So which one?

Oh. You were taken in the night. So do you know if it was on the left fork or the right fork? Do you remember, on that crossroads there's a Madonna in the middle of the street—you're supposed to kiss it...But I'm just interested, so if you could remember anything about that...I've come this far—it would be great to be able to know if it was the left street or the right street.

So, Dad...Yes, I'm coming back, but I'm here now. Dad, it's all right—listen...Okay, you can't tell me whether it's the left street or the right street of the highway?

He hung up on me! God, he bloody hung up on me! Unbelievable. 'Thank you for ringing from Poland,' he said, and hung up. *Jesus!*

After my return from Poland I did what I should have done before I went there: find out more about the places on my itinerary. Miriam Weiner's classic book *Jewish Roots in Poland* had just been published and the entry on Siedlce had a photo of the Jewish cemetery at the end of Dad's street. I learned that it had been established in 1807. In 1939 there were thirty-five thousand inhabitants of the town, nearly half of them Jewish. The town itself was founded in the mid-fifteenth century and Jews settled there a hundred years later, first as innkeepers and later as craftsmen and merchants. The town burned down at the end of the seventeenth century but it regained its position as an important commercial and cultural centre by the early eighteenth century. It fell under Austrian and then under Russian rule. A Jewish high school opened during World War I, and after the war several Jewish newspapers were active, as well as a Jewish hospital. Dad had drawn the Jewish hospital on his odd little map.

The Germans occupied the town on 11 September 1939. They burned down the synagogue on Christmas Eve that year; the ghetto was formed in August the next year, and in October it was sealed off. In August 1942 ten thousand Jews were deported to Treblinka. This must have been when Dad jumped on one of the departing trains to look for his family. Several thousand more Jews were shot in the forced-labour camp established in Siedlce. This was the camp that Dad had been working in when his brother came to take him to Bimbrowski's place.

I'd known nothing about this.

Occasionally Dad would tell me about his mother crying because she couldn't afford for him to go to high school, and he once showed me a school report that proved he had been an excellent student. He must have taken it with him to the cellar. He was apprenticed to a tailor at age thirteen and described being sent to the blacksmith's forge for coals to place in their irons for pressing clothes. Dad's stories sounded like they'd been written by the Brothers Grimm.

By the time I arrived, Siedlce was yet another shabby town in eastern Poland, in a state of neglect since the war and through the years of Soviet rule. The buildings' cast-iron balconies, which you see in old photos and which the Nazis took for making armaments during the war, had not been replaced.

Dad had never spoken about Siedlce's history: it was as if he'd arrived in a puff of smoke. When I offered to show him photographs I'd taken of his town, he was reluctant. I had to force him to look at them, and I gave up after a few minutes. He did not feel the least bit sentimental about my having gone across the world to stand in the street where he played as a child.

Searching online, I found a reference to a memoir of survival in Siedlce by Shimon Goldman, written in Hebrew.

There is an English translation, but it's in the New York Public Library and you can only look at it there. I imagined flying across the planet to read it. If this were one of the Goldman brothers with whom Dad had shared the cellar, it would be a great find. Or maybe it was another Goldman altogether?

Instead I read about what happened when the Germans took over Siedlce, organising the labour camp and death squads. The Reckmann camp was established in the town's fire station in January 1941, with barracks by the railway tracks. The labourers built and repaired the tracks, and carted coal. In March 1943 the camp was liquidated, as they say (my parents used the term, too); but before that Dad had made the journey to Treblinka and back, then gone into hiding in Bimbrowski's cellar with the Goldmans. I found accounts of other people escaping from Treblinka in the same way, saved by hiding in the piles of clothing and waiting there till the train left the station, carrying the stowaways.

One was from the Siedlce ghetto memoir of Cypora Jablon Zonszajn, who wrote her notes in an exercise book before she managed to place her eleven-month-old daughter, Rachela, with some brave and honourable Polish people, who hid her and looked after her till the war was over. Cypora took things into her own hands before she was shipped out with the others: she killed herself with poison. Her journal, reproduced online, is harrowing reading.

> The wagons are going to Treblinka. I have news from there from Maks Bigelman of Warsaw, who worked there for fifteen days (from August 27th to September

9th) sorting out belongings of those brought in, and escaped. This man is at present lodged with me and relates many things...The wagons arrive at the station of Treblinka. Here the wagons are emptied of people and belongings. The people go through the gate to the square on which are two barracks. Women and children go to the left, men to the right. The women stand before one of the barracks, the men at the other. The women take off their shoes before the entrance then go inside to undress completely. From this barrack the women go along a corridor by a garden path to the 'baths'. These 'baths' are situated in the next securely and tightly sealed barrack. Four hundred people go inside and it is locked with a horizontal bar from outside. In front of the barrack are four machine guns which 'help' them to go in. When the barrack is closed, gas is introduced...

Young people are taken from among those who stand in the first courtyard. They work at sorting out all the clothes. These clothes taken from those who have gone to 'bathe' are put into parcels, put on the wagons and sent straight back again. Thanks to these wagons a few hundred people saved themselves. It is from these that we know about everything.

After two weeks Maks had got into a wagon with items which were being sent back and in this way he made his escape.

I was taken aback by this confirmation of Dad's own escape story, which didn't need to be confirmed at all. I spent a miserable time looking at survivor testimonies, with my heart in my mouth.

And yet it was the wrong father and the wrong town, and my trip there—finding the paranoid anti-Semitic singer and suspicious neighbours—left me with no feeling of connection at all. All I'd discovered was that my parents had failed to fill out their marriage certificate. It seemed symptomatic of their life together, which was also empty of the correct information, of the flowering of love and of any remnants of empathy.

But if I'd spent that time in Mława, Max Dunne's birth-place, about 125 kilometres north-west of Warsaw, would my reception have been any different?

4

Who are you again?

I WAS haunted by the words of the older of Max's two nephews. What did he mean by Max having been made into a 'beast' by his experiences in Auschwitz? In Mama and Dad's circle of survivors, those parents who'd been in Auschwitz seemed to inhabit a special category for us kids, as though outlasting that particular circle of hell dealt you a perverse trump card. My parents had been 'in labour camps', 'in hiding' and 'with false papers' on the Aryan side. Which seemed to me to be less horrible than the experiences of those in the concentration camps. How had I worked that out? Sometimes one of my parents' friends would say or do something angry or aggressive, or break down in tears at an afternoon-tea gathering, and Mama would whisper to me 'She was in Auschwitz' as a way of explaining things.

There was also a line in the sand between Holocaust survivors and Holocaust refugees—those who had come after the war and those who had arrived in Australia before it was no longer possible to get out. Even those who came alone as refugee children and subsequently lost their families were considered the lucky ones. So, while they had both been adults before the war, there must have been a chasm between Joseph Dunne and his brother Max, five years younger, one here before the war and the other who came at the end of 1948.

I found journal articles about these hierarchies of suffering that look at populations of survivors across the globe. Again, child survivors were considered to be low in the pecking order. Was the thinking that they must have had someone looking after them, or that they couldn't remember horrible things like adults could? Or that they couldn't interpret what they were seeing, that shocking things might not be so shocking to those who didn't understand how far they fell short of a measure of humanity and civilisation?

Mama and Dad had no visible tattoos. The only evidence of their traumas was the private horror show inside their minds. They had friends with the tattooed black or navy or green numbers on their left arms, and when we asked about them we were told that it was only a way for them to remember their phone numbers. Why couldn't they remember them, I thought—I knew mine. Recently I met the father of an old Sunday school friend who told me he used to say to kids of my generation that the tattoo was his phone number, but now he tells his great-grandchildren that it's his PIN.

The adults in my parents' circle were mostly remote: they ignored us, and wanted us to play outside all the time; and they ignored their own kids, unless they were smacking them for being annoying. That was my impression, although

I never stayed overnight with any of their families, which is the only way you can see what families are truly like. But I could see that you didn't want to cross them. How much tougher could Max the beast really be?

I was in a frenzy of activity. I telephoned the daughter of Max's best friends and arranged a meeting. Once again I parked my car in a stranger's street. I approached the house with a mixture of bravado and embarrassment. In her kitchen I told my ridiculous story. I was getting adept at explaining to strangers the odd theory I had developed about my parentage. It felt like one of those dreams where you are in your nightie while everyone else is dressed. I would have been more ashamed if it were not such an intriguing tale to tell.

The daughter of Max's friends was a glamorous woman, a few years older than me. Her father had been a heroic fighter in both the 1943 Warsaw ghetto uprising and the 1944 Polish Resistance uprising in Warsaw. Would such a man befriend the Beast of Auschwitz?

Perhaps slightly shocked, she was nevertheless helpful. She told me what she could remember about Max, and that he was not so much a beast as a man who could sometimes be difficult. He had been close to her parents.

She remembered his son Alan, a handsome curly blond and blue-eyed boy, a troublemaker. She'd had a crush on him. She found a photograph of Joseph's younger son, a general practitioner now in his mid-fifties, a very good friend of hers. I looked at his face and saw echoes of my own. I was beginning to worry that I'd lost perspective, that I would see echoes of my face in any photograph, if I willed it.

She promised to ask her mother if there was any possibility of a dark secret that Max may have shared with his friends. Her mother still saw Max's widow. Perhaps the woman had talked about this scandal in the past. So many afternoon teas and dinners and parties. So many chances for whispers and raised eyebrows. If Max was difficult, his wife must have fought with him. Perhaps she confided in her friends about how hard it was to live with him. His affairs, his illegitimate child. Now I was running purely on imagination. I had to resist that and stick to what I knew.

Before I left, she said she'd try to get me in touch with Max's younger nephew and his family, who were expecting a new granddaughter. True to her word, she soon sent a message saying he was keen to meet me. I made the call. He was lovely on the phone and asked me to dinner.

The next week I was sitting at my sister's table, Dad and his wife at the head, and I felt like I was the one having an illicit affair. I looked across at him, thinking that he had nothing to do with me. I saw him merely as an instrument of my quest. It felt urgent and dangerous to ask him for clues that might help me, to breezily put questions to him without explaining why I was interested. I had taken on Mama's persona. She was the one having the affair, after all—she was the one disguising herself as a wife when she was also a mistress.

We were drinking coffee and eating cakes. 'Nothing for me,' Dad said. 'My wife says I'm on a diet.' When we pressed him, he relented. He was always happiest when he was eating, and like all survivors he ate quickly. We ate quickly, too, emulating their anxiety about the plate being taken away.

We had to learn how to eat like free people much later. His wife said nothing but shook her head. Her plate was spotless: no cake for her. But she could never be found without a cigarette dangling from her lips.

I asked Dad if he worked in the same factory as Mama did before I was born. I imagined it might have been hard to carry on a clandestine relationship with the boss if your husband was there every day.

'No,' he said, 'she worked there because her friend Isabel told her about the job, but she got pregnant a few months after taking it and stopped working. If you want to know something, ask Isabel. But she's in a nursing home after having five strokes.'

He didn't ask why I was interested in their 1950s factory experiences when I had never asked about them before. I was elated to get away with the probing and to have a new clue to follow. I imagined Mama getting pregnant only a few months after starting the new job. Nine years of infertile marriage to Dad, with visits to gynaecologists in Paris and in Melbourne—then she fell pregnant. Was her husband surprised? I know he was pleased, because I'd been told that he'd been disappointed for years that he hadn't become a father like the other men in their circle. In those days men assumed it was the woman whose works were at fault. Why should he be suspicious? What did he know of the mysteries of the female body? He was going to be a father.

We'd hardly said goodbye to the old couple at the door when I called the nursing home from my sister's kitchen to ask if Isabel was well enough to receive visitors. The nurse took the phone to her.

'It's Ramona here, Sabina's daughter,' I said. 'Do you remember me? Can I visit you?' Yes, she said, and asked me when. 'How about twenty minutes?'

I was anxious and in a rush when I stopped on the way to buy a big bunch of flowers: Christmas lilies. I had not seen Isabel or heard from her in twenty-five years.

In the car I tried to remember what I knew about her. She'd been an attractive woman with no children. She would buy us new dresses when Mama was out of money. There was a dramatic portrait of her hanging in her Carlton flat. It reminded me of Vladimir Tretchikoff's 'Green Lady', a popular interior-design feature at the time. When I found a shot of the Tretchikoff painting online, I realised that Isabel certainly didn't look Chinese. But she was sultry, like the Green Lady, and maybe that's what I remembered. She had short hair and red lips and wore a dress with layers of petticoats. Maybe she only wore the dress once, but that's the one I remember. She might as well have only ever worn that dress.

She was married to a brutal and unpleasant husband, Marek. He was an engineer, or at least that was what he did before the war. Afterwards, in Australia, he invented a new design for a steel coat hanger that could hold several suits suspended from one main vertical hook.

It didn't take off, probably because the horizontal hangers slid from the vertical one and the clothes landed on the floor of the wardrobe. I know this because my parents had a few of the prototypes he'd put aside when he started manufacturing another creation, a kind of mocha cream covered with chocolate and sitting on a thin biscuit base.

This was my idea of a great invention.

Marek used to try to touch me when he visited our house. He'd ask me to kiss him hello, as if he was offended that I hadn't already, and it seemed impolite not to. He'd leave sloppy wet smooches on my cheeks. As I got older, he would stand in doorways so that I'd have to squeeze past him to leave the room. Now I can see he was some kind of paedophile but back then I only knew it was a good idea to avoid him.

And that brings back the name of his finest invention. They were called Mocha Kisses.

Isabel was often depressed and sometimes had to be hospitalised after Marek beat her. Mama would get distressed calls from her. At other times Isabel seemed obsessed with her body. She insisted on showing us how to do exercises that would whittle down our hips. This involved sitting on the floor with our legs straight out in front of us, our arms likewise, and then we had to make our way across the room and back like that, on our bottoms. At age eleven I wasn't very interested in such activities.

These disparate memories scattered as I entered the foyer of the large nursing home and saw twenty wheelchairs arranged in a semicircle in the half-light of Sunday afternoon. Why were the residents organised like this? It was as if they had all been waiting for me to visit for twenty-five years—*you never call, you never write.* Which one was she? I searched their faces. Several of them were slumped in their chairs, heads down, beyond easy recognition. Then I looked more closely and saw Isabel, by now nearly eighty: her unmistakeable face, her body swollen and a burden, her left side inert, useless. I offered the flowers, which she couldn't hold. A nurse took them.

I asked if she remembered me.

'Sabina's girl,' she said. 'But who is your father?'

How could she have known that this was my reason for coming? It was perfect, cosmically ordained.

'That's why I'm here,' I told her. 'To find out who my father is.'

She looked puzzled. 'What is your father's name? Aron?'

I was struck by the absurdity of my answer to this woman who'd had a momentary memory lapse—she'd had five strokes, after all, according to Dad, who may have been mistaken or exaggerating. She wasn't asking me a metaphysical question.

Isabel told me to wheel her to her room, which she shared with a bedridden deaf woman who was determined not to turn her television down from its ear-blasting levels. They had a growling conversation in Polish and I sensed hatred. I wouldn't have lasted a day in this room. If I had a choice, that is, and Isabel didn't.

She directed me to push the wheelchair again and we went into the corridor to find a dark corner in which to talk. I asked if she remembered working for the Dunne brothers. She did. What were they like? 'The older one was very nice and the younger one was very handsome.' Did she remember working with Mama there? 'Yes, we worked side by side, telling each other how unhappy we were in our marriages.'

Then she asked if I knew why she'd been punished, why she was so sick and helpless. Before I could find an answer, she said, 'Because'—and now she was whispering.

I was in a labour camp working in Poland during the
war, making uniforms, and a woman who was pregnant
worked at the same bench as me. And then the time
came for her to give birth and she was terrified that
the guards would find out, and so she was working and
sewing and trying to keep her legs together and finally
she just couldn't and fell on the floor and give birth,
and the guard took the baby by the feet and flung
its head against the wall and smashed its brains out.
I vowed I would never have children and I had two
abortions after the war. And that is why I am being
punished. Because I am a murderer.

No, you're not, I whispered. No, you're not. And then I cried.
And then she cried and asked for a cup of tea. What have I
done, I thought as I brought the tea—what am I doing here,
upsetting a poor old lady and hearing horrible stories I
didn't ask for?

The tea calmed Isabel. She asked what else I wanted to
know. I asked her if she knew what Mama thought of the
younger Dunne brother, Max.

'Do you really want to know?' she said.

Yes, I said. That's why I came.

'She loved him.'

My heart missed a beat, and I breathed in deeply. I was
thrilled. I didn't want to breathe out; I wanted to savour
the moment.

I told Isabel I thought it was possible that Max was my
father.

'It's possible,' she said. 'But I was always too afraid to ask
your mother.'

I asked if Max visited Mama after she left the factory. Isabel said she thought he used to visit her in our flat during the day, when Dad was at work.

Then she slumped again in her chair and I wheeled her back to her room, where the other inmate had fallen asleep. I turned off the television. I told Isabel I'd see her again, thanked her and said goodbye.

'Who are you again?' she asked.

As I found my car I was overcome by the fear that Isabel might be an unreliable witness, drifting in and out of the here and now. *Who are you again?* But I put the thought behind me as I drove home. It was raining and bleak, yet I felt that I'd been given a precious gift.

She loved him. I could have been born out of love and not out of violence or carelessness or indifference. It seemed to matter.

But there were new problems, too. I was relying on the memories of a woman who surely had suffered brain damage from her strokes. Did her inability to remember to whom she was speaking invalidate her recollections about what Mama was up to forty-five years earlier? Did my attachment to the idea that my mother and this putative father were in love colour my ability to judge the accuracy of her information?

When I checked the records in the National Archives I saw that Isabel and her husband had arrived in Melbourne in January 1952 on the SS *Cyrenia*, so at least she was in the country at the right time. I searched for papers on mental competency and brain injuries after strokes. I read that people with intellectual disabilities or limited IQs could give evidence in court, provided they understood the question they were being asked and the need to tell the truth. Sometimes people were judged to be capable of giving unsworn evidence rather than sworn evidence. They had to able to understand things like where they were and what was wrong with them. They might have short-term memory loss but still be able to understand and remember things that happened before their brain injuries.

I thought about Isabel and the predicament she was in—she understood it and felt she was being punished. She remembered my mother and the conversations they'd had. And even if she'd forgotten who I was between my arrival and my departure, surely her story would be admissible in a court of law? Long-term memory is the last thing to go in the elderly and the demented. Isabel knew about the nice older brother and the handsome younger one. She remembered being unable to ask Mama who the father of her baby was. Most likely she'd heard that Mama couldn't conceive for nine years with Dad.

I was especially interested that she was afraid to ask Mama about her baby. My mother's silent message that enquiries were unwelcome was even directed at her friends and colleagues.

Despite my attempts to rationalise Isabel's information, I was loath to let the germ of a love story go. And this quest, this obsession, was affecting my morality. I was happy to use an old family friend as a source for my investigation and yet, though I was moved by her plight and her story about why she had no children, I did not visit her again. According to cemetery records, Isabel died eighteen months after my visit.

After my visit to the nursing home, I had thought about how Isabel saw the newborn baby being murdered. At one of the Auschwitz trials the survivor Dunia Wasserstrom described the actions of Wilhelm Boger, known as the Devil of Birkenau, who saw a child who'd just arrived at Auschwitz holding an apple. She described how Boger took the apple from the child, then killed him by smashing his head against a wall, and how, later, she saw the man at his desk eating the apple. From this moment, Wasserstrom said, she could not look at a child without crying and no longer wished to have a child of her own.

I'd heard this kind of story when eavesdropping on the conversations of survivors who were friends with Mama and Dad. Once, my mother talked about a woman they knew who went mad after the war. She had hidden with her baby and some other people, and they were at risk of being found by a patrol. The baby began to cry and the woman had to strangle it to save everyone else.

What could I do with such a story? There were no follow-up conversations about context or meaning. Had I filed away Isabel's story in the same drawer as these other terrible images? Filed it after our meeting, and moved on?

Perhaps there was little I could have done to help Isabel, anyway. I wasn't a counsellor or a psychiatrist, and she had been absent when Mama was dying, I recalled. But she was a battered woman, caught up in her own troubles.

All this was conjecture.

I was dependent for my evidence on damaged people who had been subjected to the brutal shifts of history. I needed their stories so that I could weave them into the beginnings of my own little life. Isabel's information was another piece of the puzzle—a puzzle that was starting to consume my days. To solve it I turned my attention in a different, more scientific direction.

5

My mother's taste in men

MY sister and I were sitting in big leather armchairs in her lounge room, scraping the inside of our cheeks. DNA testing kits were on our laps. We giggled as we watched each other. She was making elaborate gestures with the sampler to ensure a good specimen.

I placed them in the containers provided, added photos of us and sworn affidavits, and put them in an overnight parcel to Sydney. This was in the period before DNA testing became reasonably common. My sister was doing this as a favour to me.

Possibly she thought that my suspicions about Dad not being my real father were an elaborate fantasy that I had unconsciously concocted because I could not accept the truth: that my father *was* my father. She may have hoped that these test results would prove me incorrect and put the matter to rest. Whatever the case, I paid the $640 fee, huge at the time, and sent the parcel off on its journey into the future, and the past.

The next week I was standing before another strange

house with yet another bunch of flowers. I had bought tulips, as it was autumn. This time the door was opened by Max Dunne's younger nephew, whose blue eyes and curly hair I recognised from the photo his father had shown me. His wife welcomed me in, his children were at the table with their partners, and there was even a dog padding about. They made a lovely family picture, complete, with no obvious gaps that I could step into.

I felt overwhelmed, aware of the searching looks across my eyes and face and hair. The gap between my front teeth, which up till then I was not aware held any particular significance, was remarked upon. We all seemed keen to talk, and I listened to them speaking, to their voices, and searched their faces, too. Where did those eyes fit, that chin, that colour hair? This is what we do, I reminded myself: we classify. This is how people learn about the world, about new situations.

I told my story yet again, noticing how deft I was getting at the order, the dramas, the nuances. I was building up quite a rich portrait.

They seemed interested. They answered my questions about Max and his relationship with his wife, his brother (their father and grandfather) and Max's son, Alan.

I learned that Alan had fled Melbourne to get away from Max and to kick a heroin habit. The thought crossed my mind that I was about to swap a full sister, a rock and an upstanding member of society, for a couple of half siblings, one of whom was an ex—I hoped—junkie. I heard Dad's voice in my ear. He was fond of folk sayings: *You can pick your friends but you can't pick your relatives!*

But this group of people who were making me welcome

and feeding me were kind, and Max's nephew said he'd never had a sister or a female first cousin. He told me he was keen to claim me, if the story was true. And one of the ways we could tell if it was true was if Alan would give me a cell sample to DNA test against mine. This was a matter we would have to think about carefully, as—I was reminded—Alan was close to his mother and no one wanted to hurt any of the old people.

I imagined, too, that he'd made sure he couldn't be easily contacted. He was living on bushland outside the little mountain town of Kuranda, north of Cairns, without a phone. He didn't always answer his mail, I was told.

First, I needed to get the result from the DNA test I'd done with my sister. I promised to keep the family posted, and took my leave.

My younger daughter called me from Jerusalem, where she was doing a few subjects towards her politics degree. She'd taken an extra one in Jewish rabbinic law—Halakhah—to make up points, she said. Had I thought about the laws of *mamzerim*? These laws governed the children, the bastards, born from adulterous relationships.

Like me, I said, or my sister, or both of us.

My daughter suggested that maybe there were things we'd rather not know. Rather not know? When had there ever been anything I'd rather not know?

She reminded me that *mamzers* were forbidden to marry anyone except other *mamzerim* for ten generations. But I've only ever married bastards, I thought.

I could tell that this quest of mine had been reviewed in family conversations that I hadn't be privy to. When my sister said that Dad had been over for lunch, my daughter said, 'Oh, you mean the artist formerly known as *zayde* [Yiddish for "grandfather"]?' A joke about Prince, and about me, too.

But she was right that the semantic categories were becoming more strained. I didn't know much about the laws pertaining to bastardy: I could imagine that Mama might not have wanted to bring up the subject when I was young. I scoured the texts for the laws of *mamzerim*. So long as a couple could marry each other if they wanted to, their child was not a *mamzer*. On the other hand, if my mother was unable to marry my father, if she was already married, or if he was (as was the case with Max) or might be, then I and ten generations of my offspring would be classified as *mamzers*. It would be the same had I been the product of an incestuous coupling. Would I have to seek out a registry of *mamzers*, a dating site for *mamzers*?

So severe are the implications of this law that rabbis have found myriad ways to avoid declaring someone a *mamzer*. If there was no foolproof way of proving that an adulterous relationship had led to a pregnancy, the rabbis assumed the child was not a *mamzer*. Even if the mother declared that she thought her child belonged to a man not her husband, but she'd slept with her husband during the previous twelve months—*twelve*, mind you—the child was assumed to be the husband's. Why did rabbis make these outrageous laws and then spend centuries working out ways around them? This is what happens when you follow a set of ancient tribal principles.

The sages admitted that it was harsh to punish the children of a forbidden relationship. They also pointed out that in the next life, or in heaven, or when the messiah came, *mamzers* will be free to stand tall with the rest.

Thanks, I thought. I have never been a patient person, and I was certainly not happy to wait till the next life to be considered equal. Then why did I care what a group of excessively strict rabbis had to say on my status and my ability to marry freely? It was crazy for an educated twenty-first-century woman to care about what a small group of zealots thought of a tribal ruling many thousands of years old; all the same, I felt insulted by the law. I felt the injustice of punishing children for the faults of their parents, and miffed that I might be in the same category as those born from incestuous relationships. I felt cast aside, passed over, resentful.

Even in the age of DNA testing there were ways around a ruling. Unless it was possible to eliminate all false positives and false negatives from the results, the testing could never be used to declare *mamzer* status. And even if the testing showed that the woman's husband couldn't be the father, then the question of who the father was, and whether the father could theoretically marry the mother, was another point to debate.

My thoughts shifted to the *shtetl*, the village where Mama was born, and the Orthodox family in which she was brought up. Although she was intellectually rebellious, she still had habits from her religious childhood, such as saying a blessing over the first fruits from the trees in our garden or over new clothes. Or spitting three times if anyone said we were pretty or clever, and making us hold a piece of red cotton in our mouths when she was sewing a hem or a button on some clothing while we were wearing it—both acts to ward off the evil eye. And lighting candles on Friday nights, fasting on Yom Kippur, having a Seder at Passover. All of these were confusing habits from someone who gave us ham sandwiches for lunch, and who cooked milk and meat together.

Part of her may have recognised the seriousness of her actions, the implications for her daughters had they wished to marry into the Orthodoxy, no matter how unlikely that might have been. Would she have risked the happiness of her daughters and grandchildren (for ten generations, no less) by making an admission like this? Why would such an expert evader tell a truth so profoundly disruptive?

I came across a website offering *mamzer alerts* in which they accused some Orthodox women of coercing their husbands into giving them divorces, and subsequently remarrying. There was a ruling that, if there was coercion, the divorces were not legitimate; the alert names the women and warns men not to go out with them because, if they marry, any children of this new marriage will be considered *mamzers* till the end of time. Such was the curse of the *mamzer*, which I idly considered as I shifted my status as the daughter of Dad, the little Jewish tailor from Siedlce, Poland, to the daughter of—whom, exactly?

I rang the laboratory. The results should have come back days before. The doctor said they were being typed up at that moment. Would I like him to tell me over the phone? Yes.

I'd waited long enough for this—forty-four years, in fact—and I thought nothing could surprise me.

He talked about alleles and matches and percentages but the sentence that stayed in my mind was: 'All this says beyond a doubt is that you and your sister are half-siblings.'

As I breathed out, he said that he was never sure what to say about these kinds of results. I thanked him and said that he had confirmed what I suspected anyway.

I rang my sister and told her. She was silent. Then she said, *God, Ramona.*

She wanted to wait and get the formal results so she could read them for herself.

When the report came, I made her a copy. She read it and placed it on the table in front of me. You keep it, she said.

I was confused. She seemed surprised by the result, taken aback. This was my crusade, after all. And the DNA test merely proved that I was on the right track. Excited, my thoughts racing ahead, I left my sister in my wake.

Either I was a *mamzer* or my sister was, or maybe, if there had been two lovers involved, both of us were. One of us, for sure. But which one? And if we were from different extra-marital couplings, and Max Dunne was my father, who might my sister's father be?

She didn't want to speculate with me. I was disappointed but remembered that this was not my main interest. If my sister wanted to find out whether she was Dad's daughter, it was up to her to do so. She seemed disconcerted enough by what I had managed to discover so far.

There was another lead I needed to follow before any more of my informants died or became incapacitated. Spurred on by the DNA test, I reasoned there was no time to lose.

Mama and Dad's acquaintances included various couples that they'd met on the boat coming to Australia or in factories where they worked, or who were friends of friends. One person who I liked enormously was Mr Lederman. He would play with me, tossing me up in the air. And, more importantly, catching me. He was strong and dark, and had a full head of hair and a moustache. In the film taken at the fancy dress party in 1970 where Mama was a hippie, he appears swathed in sheets as a dashing Arab sheikh.

Mr Lederman was sometimes in our kitchen when my sister and I came home from school in the afternoon. I remember Mama once being in her dressing gown. When I asked why, she told me she hadn't been feeling well. Though Mama said nothing more, I somehow knew not to mention anything to Dad. Since we rarely talked closely with him, this wasn't a problem.

Mr Lederman worked as a builder and had been a truck driver when he arrived in Australia. He'd driven trucks in the Soviet army during the war after being taken east from Poland when the Russians arrived. Maybe he reminded Mama of the Russian soldiers who had rescued her and Dad by allowing them to hitch a ride to Berlin in 1946. He seemed less damaged than some others in Mama and Dad's circle. He'd been a business partner with my mother in a property they bought after Mama received a small sum in war reparations from Germany—an above-board reason for them to meet.

His wife had thick glasses and a nasal voice. She couldn't have children, so they had adopted a son who was a year or two younger than me and a year or two older than my sister. Mama told me that Mr Lederman's wife was not really suited to him, but he couldn't leave her as she had saved him in the war and he felt he owed her loyalty.

I was puzzled by this story. Mrs Lederman was a kind woman, a good cook and very hospitable. Once, I saw that she had set the table for a dinner party a week ahead. This was the only evidence I saw of her strategic planning, and so I wondered how a strong Red Army driver might need rescuing by her.

Did Mama really believe this was the reason they stayed together, the reason Mr Lederman could not come to her?

In the months before her death Mama had told me that Mr Lederman would be there for us in the future if we ever needed anything. Neither of us elaborated on the circumstances in which we might need him, and we didn't discuss her dying.

He arrived at my house unannounced in the weeks after her funeral, asking what Mama had told me about him. My sister remembered him visiting her some years later and saying that Mama had never told him if he was my father, because she hadn't been sure. I remember her telling me that Mr Lederman said Mama had never told him if he was *her* father, because she hadn't been sure. Her father? My father? We laughed at the madness of this conversation and our mixed-up memories.

Bern, whose phone call got me started on these explorations, had told me that she suspected Mr Lederman was my sister's father. He was swarthy. But so was Dad. And Dad had said he'd had a reddish beard. My sister had straight red hair. It was a merry-go-round. That beard, these eyes, this chin.

I decided to call him.

The last time I'd seen Mr Lederman he was wearing whites and was on his way to a tennis match with friends. He came to my front door and I asked him in for coffee. I would have been in my late twenties, he in his sixties. He sat on my couch and told me softly how much like my mother I was. At that moment, side by side on the couch—after some years in which I saw him as a substitute father, when he'd given me advice on buying the very house we were sitting in, following the collapse of my first marriage—I had the distinct impression that he was viewing me as a woman, as a desirable substitute for my deceased Mama. I ended the visit abruptly.

Now, nearly twenty years later, I called and asked him to meet my sister and me for coffee. I wanted to talk about some new information that had come to us about Mama, I said, and about what happened around the time we were conceived and born.

At first he agreed. A couple of days later he rang to cancel. He wanted to know more about what I had found, and reluctantly I told him.

'Why do you want to bring all of these things up so many years later? Will it change anything?' he asked.

I didn't even know if I'd been born when he began his relationship with Mama, I replied.

He said he didn't remember.

'Wouldn't you remember if she had a baby or not?'

We talked about what he remembered and didn't remember, and then I asked him straight if he'd ever wondered whether he was the father of me or my sister. Knowing, of course, that he'd had the conversation with my sister years ago.

'I'm not ready to consider these things,' he told me.

'How old are you now?' I asked coolly.

'Eighty-three.'

'And when exactly do you think you will be ready?'

He said he would ring again soon to arrange a meeting.

I wanted nothing from him, I said—just a story.

When you decide to do something, my sister told me, no matter if I want to know something or not, I have to know it. Everything you do affects me.

She was right. It was true and inevitable. But how could I be my mother's child from an adulterous relationship and make no waves in my sister's life? And what was the alternative: should I not pursue the questions about who I was because someone else preferred not to know?

My sister had no doubts about who her father was. Her husband brought out pictures of Dad the next time we were all at their place and compared them to his wife's face. They had no need to ask anything further. If my assumption was right and she thought that my fantasy would be shattered by the DNA test, she must have been shocked at the result. No more, she told me. You're going too fast for me.

A few days later old Mr Lederman called again. This time he said he didn't want to meet me, and that he was uncomfortable and would only talk to me on the phone.

He was *uncomfortable.*

I thought of the months I spent caring for Mama as she died. She wanted to see Mr Lederman. They'd fallen out months earlier, when Dad left home to live with his girlfriend and didn't contribute to my sister's upkeep. She was a full-time student, and Mama was sick and couldn't work. Mama asked Mr Lederman to approach Dad's boss to see if some of his wages could go directly towards supporting my sister. Mr Lederman refused. He wasn't ready for his relationship with Mama to be that public. They argued and she asked him to leave the house.

When I heard her ask for him again during a conversation with Bern, there was a joke about whether she'd ever taken anyone's husband, and she said she'd never stolen one but had borrowed a few. Such openness was rare for Mama. It may only have been possible because she was talking to Bern, and maybe the morphine had lowered her guard.

Bern told Mr Lederman that Mama was asking for him, but he never came to see her. He arrived in the evening of the day of her funeral, at the *minyan*, the gathering in the house of the deceased at which you recite prayers for the dead. She was long past needing him. I wonder now what she'd wanted to say.

Here he was on the end of a phone line, not a silver fox shining in his white tennis gear, but a rather fearful old man in the face of my questions.

I asked him if he remembered how Mama was in those

early years in Australia after the war: an orphan, a displaced person; poor, uneducated, unhappy. Was she depressed?

He had no idea. They didn't talk about personal things. He was only her partner in a minor business transaction.

But, I said gently, she loved you.

'Who told you that?'

She did.

'Lots of people liked me, I hope.'

But you were her lover.

'No, I was not. We were just business partners.'

Mama, Mama, how sad I felt then. That he denied you after all those years. That he'd forgotten his own conversations with me years before, when he'd asked what Mama had told us about him. That he'd forgotten my seeing him with Mama in her dressing gown that afternoon years earlier.

Bern remembered that he'd been a fixture in Mama's life from the time she met Mama at the kindergarten which her son and my sister attended, and that she herself had interrupted them one afternoon when she had dropped in at our house unannounced. *Business partners*. How cowardly.

I said goodbye to Mr Lederman, telling him that Mama had said that if we ever needed anything, he would be there to help us.

'Yes, of course.'

But, I thought, not for this. I hung up the phone and sat at the bay window, staring at the leaves falling in the wind. It was almost winter out there, and it felt like it.

When I told my sister about the conversation, she asked me what I'd really expected of a man who refused to visit

Mama as she lay dying. He'd told my sister afterwards that at the time he hadn't believed Mama was so sick.

Years later I found the cemetery records for Mr and Mrs Lederman. She died seven years after my call to him, and he died eleven months after her. They were buried side by side.

He had eleven months to get in touch with me after his wife was safely out of the picture, if that was why he'd been so coy and untruthful with me. But he never did. Nor was there a letter to be opened after his death. Maybe he was too sick or demented to arrange such a thing.

Mr Lederman left me no note and neither did Max. I was beginning to doubt my mother's taste in men.

6

Who's going to pay?

DAD pointed at the dishes spread across the lunch table, shaking his head. There were salads and dips, and smoked salmon with capers, and cream cheese and bagels, and fruit and cakes.

'I was brought up by a herring and a couple of onions,' he announced.

Later I repeated his strange syntax to my sister, unable to control my laughter. This explains a lot, I said through my tears. Maybe my real father was a herring and a couple of onions, too?

I was on my own in this. My heightened hysteria found meaning in the slightest of conversational transactions. Everything was possibly something when there was almost nothing to go on.

10 June 1999

Dear Alan,

What a strange call you've just had from your cousin, you must be a bit puzzled. And I certainly don't want to make your life more complicated or disturb you in any way. But recently I've been doing some investigations into a story I've been wondering about for some time. It's a pretty long story which I'll cut short for the sake of clarity, but there are quite a few things which lead me to believe that it's possible that your father Majlech was my father too. Which may make me your half-sister.

My mother Sabina (Sara) was a Jewish survivor from Poland who worked for your father and your uncle at Dunne Brothers in 1953. She was unhappily married to another Jewish survivor and had been trying to have children for nearly nine years unsuccessfully. After working for your father for some months, she became pregnant and left the factory. I was born in the middle of 1954.

She died of leukaemia in 1977 at the age of forty-nine, and with her died the possibility of asking her directly about my paternity. But for all of my childhood I was aware that there was a secret and that it concerned the identity of my father. Recently a close friend of my mother's told me about your father meeting the friend at an auction in Kew quite a few years ago and recognising her from when my mother used to go with her to your father's factory to buy wholesale suits.

She remembers the man at the auction asking about my mother, who had died, and then asking her many questions about me. What was I doing? What kind of work did I have? Did I have children? Was I happy? She said he seemed very pleased and impressed that I worked for the ABC [at the time I was doing a daily current-affairs talkback program]. This was all very strange because I can't remember ever meeting your father. Why did he show such interest? Then my mother's friend told me that if I wanted to find out more about my paternity, she thought that following up the Dunne connection would be fruitful, although she never knew for certain, but she suspected something.

Since then I have had confirmation from another source that my mother was in love with your father, and that they at least had a relationship which lasted till after I was born. He used to visit her in her flat in Beaconsfield Parade, St Kilda. The man I grew up with as my father knows nothing of all this, and I expect that your mother doesn't either, although I may be wrong. I certainly don't want to upset any of the old folks.

Everyone I know (including your cousin and his kids) says that I bear a strong resemblance to the photograph of Majlech as a young man. I'm tall and have curly dark-blond hair and blue eyes. I look much more like your family than any of the ones I've thought of as mine. I have two grown daughters—one nearly twenty-four, and the other twenty-one.

My sister and I have just had a DNA test done which confirms that we did not have the same father, and so are half-sisters.

It's a simple procedure which just involves scraping the inside of the cheek with a cotton bud supplied by the laboratory—no blood required.

I'd like to ask you to think about this. They tell me that the only way to find out if Majlech was my father is to compare your cells with mine. Possible first cousins are not closely enough related to say for sure.

If you agree to help me with this mystery, I'll take all responsibility for the costs involved. I'm happy to

come up to Kuranda anytime and meet you to talk
in detail and perhaps to take the sample. (I used to
be a geneticist and microbiologist before I was a
journalist.)

You can call me reverse charges, or write to me,
or send me an email.

So, when you have time to digest all this, please
let me know what you think. I know it must come as
a shock.

But then again, I was delighted to hear that you've
heard me on Radio National for some time, and so
you know something about me and hopefully the way
I think and the integrity with which I work and live
my life. I have no need to disrupt your life, or that of
your mother, or any of your family. I'm not interested
in anything beyond establishing my origins.
Yours sincerely,
Ramona

The absurdity of waiting for the nod from a stranger in a
northern backwater before I could continue my pursuit
did not escape me. I could have progressed on another tack
by getting a sample from Dad and confirming if either my
sister or I was his issue, as they say.

Some years ago, she said, my sister had asked Dad if he'd
ever considered that he might not be our father. I'm not sure
why she did this, but it may have been after a phone call or
visit from one of Mama's old friends. Dad was flabbergas-
ted, she said. He'd never considered such a thing and found
it ridiculous.

I wondered how much denial there might have been in Dad's response. Mama had told me how desperate to be a father he'd become by the time I was born. They'd fought each time her period arrived. Such was the urgency of his need, perhaps he banished all doubts he might have had about my blondness and curly hair and blue eyes.

Dad was the sole survivor from his family. His marriage to Mama was unhappy. At least he had two daughters to boast about and to assuage his manly pride.

Now we knew he couldn't be the biological father of both of us. And that he might not be the father of either. Telling him and testing him might leave him without any relatives—save for his devoted second wife, her daughter and son-in-law, and their two sons, who seemed to make him happy. Would it be right to do such a thing?

If Alan agreed to be tested, and proved to be my half-brother through Max, the story of Mr Lederman and Mama and Dad belonged to my sister. It would be hers to pursue if she chose to. I hoped Alan would agree.

A few weeks later the phone rang seconds before I was about to leave the house. Beeps indicated an interstate call; they stopped, and I said hello. Silence. I said hello again.

It's Alan from Kuranda, he said.

Ah, Alan, thanks so much for calling me, but give me your number and I'll call you back.

No, he said, don't worry. I'm in a public phone box. I don't have a phone or any electricity.

So ring me again reverse charges.

No, really, he said. If we keep arguing about who's going to pay...

And then he said: You may be my sister, so I can spend a few dollars on you after nearly fifty years.

This seemed to be a good beginning. It was tinged with warmth and acceptance. But I had been wrong about the warmth of men many times before.

I thanked him for responding to what must have been a strange letter to receive.

Why wouldn't someone respond? he said.

He'd love to meet me, he continued, but he wouldn't be coming to Melbourne in the near future.

I'd come up there, I replied. When would be convenient?

Anytime—just write to tell him.

Mid-July might be a good time. I'd stay in a motel in Kuranda and he could come in to find me.

He said that he'd listened to me on the radio and read my newspaper column and had thought what a clever girl I was. *Girl*. Maybe he used that word because I was becoming his little sister. *Clever girl*. I liked that. I needed that. How did this stranger know?

I told him how kind his family had been: even his older cousin had been open and had sent me the photo of Max. Did the cousin know this story? Alan asked. I hesitated, and in the hesitation he said: It's okay if he does.

I said yes, he knew, but I hadn't spoken to him for months and all of the recent contact was with Alan's younger cousin. I said that I knew the older cousin didn't get on with Max, and Alan said he didn't get on with a lot of people.

I hoped that family politics was not going to deflect me from my task—but Alan reiterated how much he was looking forward to meeting me. He said he'd been looking at my photo in the paper and trying to imagine me without all the curly hair. I said I'd send him up a better photo and he said he'd send me one of himself. I said I'd let him know when I was coming and he said that sometimes it was a week between visits to the post office and he might take some time to respond.

We said *see you soon.*

And I hung up and rejoiced that another door was opening.

I booked two nights at the Kuranda Rainforest Resort for what happened to be my forty-fifth birthday. I would fly up using frequent-flyer points in just under a month.

In the meantime I rang the DNA laboratory in Sydney for advice about the testing. The doctor said that because I was female and Alan male it would be best to exclude his mother's genome: could I get her to give a sample, too? No, I could not.

This would necessitate testing for ten or fifteen different alleles, costing another thousand dollars. I'd been a single mother for many years, supporting two daughters on a public broadcaster's salary, and had little savings. This was getting expensive for what might prove to be a folly, but I felt I had to persist.

On the treadmill at the gym later that morning I remembered that Alan had a daughter. Maybe she could substitute for his mother's genes. She'd have his X chromosome, which he'd got from his mother. I wasn't sure what would happen with the rest of the chromosomes, the autosomes. I couldn't remember the genetics I'd studied twenty-five years before, but I did remember wanting to study genetics because I was fascinated by the way looks were transmitted from one generation to the next—though not in my family.

I was the only one with curly hair. Dad had straight black hair, my sister had lovely straight red hair, and Mama's hair was brown and slightly wavy. Mama said that when she was a little girl she had curls just like mine, but then they went straight and her hair turned brown.

From what I knew about the way these things go, I expected that a child of Dad's would have straight dark hair. Mama said that Dad's beard was reddish and that was why my sister's hair was reddish, too. 'Isn't that right?' she'd ask him, projecting the question into the space between them rather than speaking directly to him. And he would nod: yes, a red beard, that's right.

Alan called from the phone box again to say he'd meet me at the airport in Cairns and drive me to the hotel in Kuranda. He seemed as excited as I was. He told me that he and his partner had seen the photograph I'd sent, and I looked even more like Max than he did.

And he said that he remembered vividly a time when he was about five and his mother kicked his father out of their Carlton house. His memory was of looking out through the venetian blinds in the front window and seeing his father with a suitcase in his hands. Years afterwards, when his father was dead, Alan asked his mother what the fight was about. She told him that his father had been having an affair.

I was born when Alan was almost five years old.

I was beside myself with excitement on hearing this. Our stories were beginning to meld into each other's. What were the odds that a stranger's story would fit into the gaps left in mine? And only seven months after Dad's eightieth birthday and the start of my search...

A couple of weeks later Alan rang again, just as he said he would, checking that our plans for the coming Friday were still on track. He told me not to worry, that he and his partner and their daughter were looking forward to meeting me.

He was making me feel wanted. Perhaps he saw me as a lost orphan. Perhaps he recognised the feeling himself.

I asked if there was anything from Melbourne that they wanted me to bring. I'd thought of cakes and chocolates from Acland Street in St Kilda: perhaps he hankered for the sweet things of childhood?

He said to leave my worries behind. Was that what he did when he left for the north? I wasn't worried, I replied, and I was keen to meet everyone. He said they had read my novel and loved it. He mentioned the Fruit Salad Farm, near Melbourne, which I had called the Strawberry Farm in the book. We laughed at the idea of all those unfit Jewish survivors walking to the top of the small hill and rewarding themselves with huge helpings of strawberries and cream.

It was odd to feel so warmly towards a man I'd never met. And there was danger in feeling too connected too fast. I had to be careful of falling in too deep out of a pathetic need to belong, the way newborn ducklings imprint their mother projections on the first thing they set eyes upon after hatching.

7

The exact same shade as mine

I FLEW from Melbourne to Sydney to Brisbane and, at last, to Cairns. A wall of tropical heat hit me as I stepped off the plane to the tarmac, and clung on as I continued down covered walkways into the waiting area.

I saw Alan but looked away, not ready to meet his eyes. He was surprisingly small and wiry, with cropped hair and a little vertical stripe of grey beard and a blond-grey moustache, and an earring in his left ear. He was dressed completely in black, and I could see ropey veins under the skin of his arms, which had been baked in the Queensland sun, like clay. He looked like the survivor of a city drug scene, which is exactly what he was.

He came up to me, spoke my name, and kissed me on the cheek. We each looked into identical blue eyes. I noted the shape of his face. I was surprised that I was taller than him and much sturdier in build. It was as if he could read my mind: he said he was thin now because he was a vegetarian and did a lot of physical work with his four horses.

We found his truck and I climbed into the cabin,

peeling off layers of clothing from the southern winter. I looked surreptitiously at his arms and hands, his nose and profile.

He was talking about horses. Reading them, their body language; what you can learn about how they communicate between themselves. He worked sometimes as a horse whisperer, he said. He and his part-Maori partner and their daughter lived quiet lives in the rainforest.

He coughed and smoked and said he had a lung condition because of what he'd been through in his life, which he'd tell me about later. I guessed it was to do with his heroin addiction, but said nothing. I knew he'd hidden himself away up here and I couldn't predict his reaction to me already knowing this about him.

I was feeling bulky next to him as I glanced at my well-covered thighs next to his skinny shanks. I realised that part of me had wanted a towering strong brother, like my image of his father. But I was the towering strong one. He must have sensed me looking him over. He told me he was wiry but strong. Either he really was reading my mind or he'd learned something valuable about non-verbal communication from horses.

He'd adopted the northern habit of saying 'ay' at the end of some sentences. His vocabulary was alternative, a hippie-dope lexicon. But he was bright and on the ball and intensely interested in the story I had come to tell him.

I began the tale as we drove the twenty kilometres to Kuranda, through the dense green bush, across rivers, all of which I hardly noticed. He quoted from parts of my novel that he thought might not have been strictly fictional.

He was an attentive listener, he assured me, and he said 'wow' and 'gee' and 'I bet' to encourage me as I told the story. He told me again how much he'd looked forward to my visit.

We were interrupted by our arrival at the Rainforest Resort on the edge of the Atherton Tablelands and my checking in. The staff there knew him and were friendly, calling out 'Hi, Al' when they saw him. I picked up the thread as we made our way to the cabin on stilts at the edge of the property, next to a wired enclosure where a family of kangaroos was housed.

Another person called out a greeting and I asked why everyone seemed to know him. In the early days—fifteen years before, when Kuranda was not yet a tourist town—he used to cut quite a figure when he rode into town, he said, and everyone knew him as 'the guy on the horse'. A better horse to be on, I thought, than heroin, the Big H.

We made tea for me and instant coffee for him, and took our cups on to the small veranda. We sat and we talked. I finished the story. He told me he thought I had been courageous. Hours passed in deep conversation. He went to the car to get his chest medication and brought back a bottle of champagne. I thought then that I must have passed some test. I had been horse-whispered.

We went inside when darkness began to fall. It was pleasant for me but it was winter here and Alan found the nights shivery without any body fat to warm him. We sat at the little table and I showed him photos of my daughters. I read him parts of my notebook, and we drank the champagne, and I produced two joints a colleague had given me a few weeks back.

He asked me what I wanted to know about him and seemed relieved when I told him I knew he had been addicted to heroin. Who told you? he asked, and I hesitated, trying to remember. He took this as an indication that I might not want to reveal my source. I told him I couldn't remember if it was his younger cousin or the family friend, and he smiled. He said that his parents were always worried about people finding out about him when clearly a lot of people already knew anyway.

He told me his story. Sometimes it intersected with mine.

Here are my notes: *Flat 1, 326 Beaconsfield Parade, St Kilda.* This was my address, the first one I learned by heart as a child, in case I got lost. According to poor Isabel in the nursing home, it was here that Max visited Mama and me when Dad was at work.

Alan remembered the ponies in the Catani Gardens on Beaconsfield Parade, next to the beach. I remembered them, too. We used to ride them, led by their handlers, round and round the small track. I liked to feel their bristly manes. On Sundays, Max took Alan to the gardens and it was there that Alan learned to love horses. He remembered, as I did, the swings and the slides and the daisies for making chains. Maybe, he said, they met in the park on a Sunday, Max with his five- or six-year-old son, and Mama with her little daughter. His daughter, too?

Then Alan remembered that Beaconsfield Parade elicited a fiery response from Max much later on, when Alan said he wanted to be near the sea in a rental place on that street. 'Why would you want to live there? What for?'

his father said angrily, and they fought about it. We agreed that it was a much more heated response to a street address than seemed reasonable. Alan thought Beaconsfield Parade must have been a trigger for him. Perhaps it was the scene of other memories?

Alan told me again about his parents splitting up for a few days when he was five. His mother found out that his father had been having an affair. So you took him back? Alan asked her years later, and she said yes, but it took her years to forgive him. Then he asked if she really had forgiven him. He couldn't remember if she answered.

Perhaps his mother knew the identity of this other woman. But did she know that the woman was carrying Max's child? And how much forgiveness would that have taken?

I pondered whether this was all coincidence. A stranger had an affair in the same period that I was conceived and born. He was touchy about a street in St Kilda where I lived for the first six years of my life. Wouldn't he be touchy about his son living in a notoriously seedy suburb rife with drug deals? Was Max just one of thousands of men in Melbourne who had affairs at the end of 1953 and through 1954? Who could answer these questions?

There was little time for speculation. I was in Kuranda for two nights, and I wanted to find out from Alan what Max was like. A child's-eye view of the man in question, as much as that was possible.

Alan says his father loved him. But that after the age of thirteen he was a great disappointment to his father. Would he have been proud of me? Is that why he asked Bern what work I did and if I was married and if I had children and if I was happy?

*Max was tall, and strong and handsome. He was a very
natty dresser. Alan has photographs taken after the war
of his father standing with a Greek Jew he knew and they
both look like they were in the Mafia. His father may have
killed a couple of people 'afterwards'—after Auschwitz,
for retribution.*

May have killed a few people? A few? How did Alan know?
Was my real father capable of murder? And how would this
make me feel: threatened, protected, proud?

*Max was a hard man. He was physically able to be violent, but he
never hit his wife or his son. He once bashed up a man in a pub who
had insulted him.* I liked the idea of a strong man, my father
being able to take down a man who'd insulted him. He
would have been able to protect me, too. But he didn't.

*Max was obsessed with anything to do with the Holocaust.
History. Biography. He read Solzhenitsyn. When there
was a program on the history of the SS on television he
would set himself up half an hour early in front of the
TV set, organised for the big night. His wife would leave
the room and sit in the kitchen with her fingers in her ears.
Alan thinks something terrible happened to her during the
war. She was in the Majdanek camp. She was five years
older than Mama.*

Max was trying to understand what had happened long
after it was over. But maybe it was never really over for him.
I thought of his wife with her fingers in her ears. Mama
didn't want to see the pictures and hear the raised German
voices either.

Max loved his wife, says Alan. More so than she loved him. We talked about the possibility of his affair with Mama being about sex rather than love. Who knows? Isabel said that Mama loved Max. Maybe she did. Or maybe she loved the idea of rescue. I once heard her remind Dad in an argument that he had promised to carry her in his arms for the rest of her life. She laughed at the thought of this. He didn't rescue her, and neither did Max.

Max loved chocolates. He loved to go to Acland Street on a Sunday morning and buy sweet things to eat. I love chocolates, too. I'd thought of bringing Alan cakes from Acland Street. Maybe Max and I could have gone together to Acland Street to buy beautiful cakes and sweet chocolates. But lots of people like chocolates and cakes. That's why there are shops full of them, and why there are chocoholics and desserts called Death by Chocolate.

Max had lung cancer, for which he had an operation. Then he had adrenal cancer which killed him. I should look up the familial patterns of adrenal cancer.

Max told his life story to a South African man he knew when he was in the hospital. It may have been Vimy in Kew. Alan can't remember the man's name. Zoshu? How could I find a South African whose name might be Zoshu? I lived near that hospital in the time that Max was dying. Maybe I drove straight past it as he was taking his last breath?

Max could get angry and throw furniture around, smashing things. It was frightening. He could rip his own shirt off when he was full of fury. Alan grabs his own shirt and mimes tearing it from the collar,

*popping the buttons, and ripping it backwards over
each shoulder.*

I imagined crouching behind the couch with Alan, waiting for the storm to pass as Max ripped the shirt off his
shoulders.

> *Max said he had blond curly hair as a child. He had grey-
> blue eyes. After the war his hair went dark, and he wore
> it slicked back like an Italian. He always wore sharp suits.
> He was hopeless at doing repair jobs around the house.
> He employed people to do this.*
>
> *Max was upset and appalled when Alan told him
> of the suggestions (from whom?) that his behaviour in
> Auschwitz may have been something of which to be
> ashamed.*
>
> *He was a tailor and he made uniforms. Then he
> got 'a good job', where he got more food. This was
> working in the infirmary.*

Where they did medical experiments? I asked. Alan said
he'd never thought about that. He didn't know.

Max was quiet. His wife was louder, a party girl...attractive,
outgoing. Mama was quiet and dignified and proud. Maybe
she suited Max better?

> *Max and his brother Joe didn't get on. Max and his
> older nephew were sworn enemies. Max called him
> a bad seed.*
>
> *Max told Alan of the reception he received on
> arrival in Australia. He expected warmth from his*

older brother Joe, as the only survivor of the family.
His brother was cool.

   (A bush turkey lands on the rail of the porch as
I write, pecks and moves on.)

   Joe was very proud of the solid-walnut dining
table in his home. Max asked him, 'What year did
you buy the table and what did you pay for it?' Max
was furious that his brother could have bought the
table in the year that the money could have been
used to rescue some of the family from Poland.
Max always said that the table represented their
sister.

I imagined the atmosphere around the table at family
dinners. I saw Joe and his family waiting for the moment
when Max's seething temper would erupt. I wondered if his
wife would put her fingers in her ears then, too.

   Alan said that it would have been just like Max to go
   to an auction in Kew, around the area in which they
   lived. And it would have been in character for him to
   be interested in what kind of work I was doing. And
   pleased at the answer. 'Sounds like Max,' says Alan.

Wallabies were padding about, thirty feet from where I was
writing. Lush tropical ferns, an avocado tree, palms, poinset-
tia, bananas. Lots of birds. In the neighbouring cabin, a young
father and his daughter of twelve or thirteen were horsing
around. He was teasing her; she teased him back. She belted
him playfully on the bum; he pushed her hand away. 'Dad!
Dad! I want to show you something!' He was laughing and

saying, 'You tone yourself down.' They bantered. I was transfixed, fascinated by the warmth between them.

On the other side of my cabin, the wallaby family were
now under the shade shelter, eating together. The father in
the next cabin had taken off his shirt. He had a star-shaped
tattoo on his left forearm.

How casual people were about tattoos now. When I was
growing up tattoos were a source of shame, especially for
women. They were a reminder that people had been viewed
as livestock, losing their names and being recorded only
by numbers.

Alan says Max never hid his Auschwitz tattoo, that he was proud
of surviving. The number was 76200. I wondered if the seven had
a line through it. That was how my parents' card-playing
friends used to write their sevens on the scoring records I
found next to piles of matchsticks on the Saturday mornings after their games.

Alan says the tattoo was on the top of his forearm, not on the
inner arm. Max said that he was one of the earlier inmates. Did they
decide later to tattoo the inner forearms?

We had finished the bottle of champagne, eaten
vegetarian pizzas and shared a joint. By eight, five hours
after I arrived, I was dead tired. Alan kissed me on the cheek,
hugged me and went off into the night. I collapsed onto the
bed. I couldn't read, couldn't think, and fell into a deep sleep.

When I woke the next morning to the sound of kooka-
burras, alone in the holiday resort on my forty-fifth birthday, I was not unhappy.

I was to wait for Alan to pick me up and take me to
the bush block where he lived. He wanted to introduce

me to his partner. Their relationship was strained. She was unhappy and pregnant and wanted to split up. They lived on her property, he'd said, but he'd being working it hard for years. He was keen for me to meet their little daughter.

Alan told me that when his younger cousin had called and left the first phone message, he was worried. He thought it might have been about his mother. When he rang back, his cousin said, 'This might sound strange but you might have a half-sister.' Tell me more, Alan replied, intrigued. He'd just been listening to me on the radio. She doesn't want anything from you, he was told, just some information.

I haven't got anything, Alan said, feeling annoyed that his cousin thought he needed reassurance on that front. Shades of relatives turning up, out of Poland, wanting things.

Someone was playing clarinet in a nearby cabin, practising their scales. I thought that, even if Alan didn't turn up that morning, the trip had already been worthwhile, and somehow settling.

The day before, I'd read Alan sections of my notebook about the meeting with Isabel. Then I remembered that there was something she didn't want me to tell anyone. I asked Alan to promise not to say anything about this section. I never promise, said Alan, but I won't tell anyone.

He never promises. I'd never met a man who'd said that. What Isabel didn't want me to repeat was not written there anyway, and I kept it to myself. I've since forgotten what it was.

Alan had told me that he was not hiding from the police or the underworld here in the remote reaches of the country. He described how, a long time ago, he'd brought hashish from Goa into Australia by eating glad-wrapped pellets of the drug and shitting them out in the shower. A fortune just sitting there. And how a Lubavitcher group had got him off heroin on a rehabilitation farm where there were horses.

He'd worked in a menswear shop. He'd had an antiques shop called Paradox. He'd worked in Cairns, too, in restaurants, washing dishes. He'd had jobs as a gardener.

I thought of what a paragon of respectability I had been. Good at school, earnest at university; marriage, motherhood; divorce-hood and single-motherhood—all the time working at universities, at freelance journalism and in public broadcasting, living frugally and paying my way. As adults, our paths never crossed in the years we lived in the same city. And here I was, making a connection with Alan of such an intimate kind. I was sharing stories with him, sharing an offer of blood.

The clarinet player was practising 'Silent Night, Holy Night'—Christmas in mid-July for a Melbourne Jew in the heat of northern Queensland. In a day's time I'd be back on a plane and headed home.

As the clock headed towards noon, they arrived. Alan with a big cake box; his little daughter holding a bunch of red and yellow flowers, asters, some daisies, big solid red tropical flowers with leaves like hearts; and his partner, visibly pregnant in a wine-coloured crushed-velvet top with a present in her hand, a bottle of herb-scented body oil.

They hugged me and wished me well for my birthday. The cake was revealed: an enormous chocolate mud cake with thick curls of chocolate on top. Had I told Alan that I love chocolate like Max did? Or had he assumed that every-one loves chocolate like Max did?

Alan handed me a plastic bag full of photographs of Max and said that I should keep them because they were at risk of perishing in the humidity. It felt like he had accepted my unlikely tale. Was I to become the keeper of Max's story?

We set up at the table on the veranda—the cake, the sparklers they had brought—and they sang 'Happy Birth-day'. We drank tea, and looked at the old photographs and took new ones, a new little family together for the first time in the tropical light.

We talked. A couple of hours went by and then we piled into his truck for a quick lunch in town. He introduced me to people there as his sister. Afterwards we got back into the truck, his daughter clutching the blue teddy bear I had brought for her, holding my hand.

The road back to their homestead crossed several small creeks and the Barron River, which they said could flood badly in the wet season, trapping them in or out for weeks. The trick was to always have plenty of provisions. The rough road would run with rivers of mud and the old four-wheel-drive was the only vehicle that could get through it. Getting bogged meant they had to use the ancient tractor, and its brakes were faulty.

Thirty minutes out of Kuranda, the homestead's yard loomed before us on a ridge. We opened the gate and closed it behind us, driving towards an open shed on two levels, one a step above the other. The weather was kept out in winter by clear plastic blinds on two sides. The rest of the place was open, and on the upper level were two beds, a chest of drawers and a central wood burner.

They had an old couch and chairs, an upright stove and a fridge (both of which ran on gas cylinders), a tank for water and a long table at which Alan sat and rolled a joint. We made blackberry tea and ate more chocolate cake.

Alan's pride and joy were the four horses he'd reared and trained, which were standing in a paddock next to the house. His daughter showed me her favourite and Alan introduced me to the one he called his best friend. They were glossy and healthy compared with the other horses that stood nearby. These belonged to his partner's ex, who lived in Port Douglas and who rarely got down to look after them. You could see their bones.

Alan saw me looking at the other horses and said it hurt him to see them like that but he couldn't afford to take care of them. I thought to myself that I could not bear to see them looking so thin. There was some kind of dispute between this couple and her ex, and the horses were caught in the middle of it.

As night fell Alan drove me back to the resort, and I waved to his partner and child though the rear window as we set off over the ridge. When we arrived he bought himself a beer and me a whisky at the bar. We'd been disputing who would pay for things for two days, both of us wanting to treat the other. Mostly I won. I was working and had more money.

These days, Alan said, he lived by picking up itinerant work like tractoring, gardening and building jobs. Things were getting harder. They lived simply and cheaply but they would feel the strain shortly with the new baby. His partner did everything by hand—cleaning, washing, cooking—and they lived by the light of petrol lamps and candles, like nineteenth-century pioneers.

We drank and I told him of my work, my travels and the trip to Poland, and I was pleased as he marvelled at my tenacity in following seemingly ridiculous leads. He told me that Max would have been immensely proud of me and that, while he could only disappoint his father, I would have made him happy.

This too pleased me. I was vulnerable enough to be pleased by the notional pride of a stranger. When he left for home, I looked at my notes again.

Alan certainly had been a troubled child. *He was only eight when he began stealing things (money, chocolates) from shops, and from his parents. He was an expert at making the chocolate jar look like it was full, when it was really nearly empty. It was a matter of architecture—building a house of cards.* I thought about how I'd been living inside a house of cards.

He liked jumping off the roof with an open umbrella. Lots of kids imagine doing this at some point, but most see that it wouldn't work. Maybe even then he liked the thrill, the rush, with no thought of the consequences of landing.

> *He brought home terrible reports from school and his father would read them and then hurl them down the corridor of the house. Alan became adept at changing the marks on the report. If you got twenty per cent, this could be changed to better than forty per cent. He got his pens and blotted the reports with ink and made the changes. The hard part was changing them back for the teachers.*

A consummate forger. In a spelling test in Grade One I tried to change my spelling of 'aeroplane' to 'eroplane' by rubbing out the 'a' so hard that I made a hole in the paper. I learned that often the first answer which comes to you is the correct one.

> He used to get onto the roof and crunch the tiles with his boots.
>
> Max would rant and rave and make him promise not to break the tiles. The next day Max would come home to see Alan on the roof again, crunching the tiles again. He asked the boy to come down.
>
> No, he'd say, you'll hurt me.
>
> Come down and I won't hurt you, I promise.
>
> No, you'll hit me.
>
> I promise I won't.
>
> And the boy came down. And the father hit him, and kicked him hard.
>
> My father never hit me, says Alan, till I was thirteen years old. Then he sometimes laid into me, and would catch himself out of control, and then stop.

So, Max did hit Alan. Dad hit me, too. Once, when I was ten, my sister and I were talking to each other after lights-out and he burst into our room in a fury, slapping me hard as I cowered under the blankets. Shapes of his hand were imprinted on my body for days after. Mama hit me, too, sometimes with a belt. Maybe everyone was getting slapped around in those years.

> My father, says Alan, would suddenly seize up with anger.
> We might be driving and you'd see the look on his face turn

*to rage. He must have been thinking about something
that made him angry, and his hands would tense up
on the steering wheel.*

*Max was proud of the numbers on his arm.
When he met people, he'd deliberately roll up his
sleeve and have his number showing—76200.*

*The photograph Alan likes best of Max is one
of him in Germany after the war, still thin, leaning
against a gate or something, his arm across his chest,
the number facing outwards.*

This was one of the photos that Alan gave me for safekeeping.

*Alan stole a bicycle and was on his way to throw it
in the river when his mother came down the street:
Where did you get the bicycle?
A boy gave it to me.
Why did he give it to you?
Because he likes me.
The eight-year-old boy stole a tuba from the
school. It was half his size. He told his parents he
had been put into the band. At night he tried to
blow it in his room. His mother rang the school
and found that he had stolen it.*

*Alan is voted sports captain and captain of
the football team. His father says, Better you
should be captain of mathematics.*

I thought about how good I was at mathematics. But not
good enough for Max to have been a proper father to me.
Was he a proper father to Alan?

Max was frightened, or cowed at least, by men in uniforms—

policemen, parking inspectors. *He was struck dumb by them, he looked down and away from their gaze.*

He liked a good joke but would never tell one. Unlike Dad, who would always tell them, often the same ones, over and over again.

Max was never depressed. He was filled with rage. What might he have made of me, if he had left his wife and Alan and come to Mama? Would Alan have been an athlete, a happy, strong and handsome devil—would I have been the one to turn to heroin?

Would I have cowered in the face of his rage? How would he have managed my questioning, my radicalism? He voted Liberal. He was fond of Richard Nixon. He and Mama would have fought bitterly about Vietnam. I wonder if she kept her secret to protect me from the man filled with rage.

The following morning I packed my things. I had a few hours before I had to head to the airport. The next day I would be having breakfast with a cultural attaché in Canberra. Two weeks later I would fly to Lake Como in Italy for a holiday with friends, then to Edinburgh to interview writers at the book festival. It was a very different life to that of Alan in Kuranda. And to Max. And to Mama. I kept thinking of the image of Max's strong forearm with the numbers proudly displayed: 76200. The survivor.

Alan and his little family arrived mid-morning. I hadn't mentioned DNA testing during my visit. Alan brought up the subject, saying it was my call. He said he was happy to believe the story I'd told, but equally happy to submit to a test.

I took out the swabs, filled in the forms, got him to sign the letter I'd written from him to the doctor, and showed him how to scrape the sampler along the inside of his cheeks. I had the urge to do it myself, to make use of my years of laboratory experience, but it seemed too intimate, and maybe too rude. The sample and the forms and the signed letter went into my suitcase.

He drove me back to the airport in Cairns. On the way, he said that Max went back.

To where?

To Auschwitz.

It was the late 1960s. At the gate a woman offered him a map. I don't need it, he said. I was here before. I know where everything is.

I told Alan that when I went there I took a recorder and a large stereo microphone on a boom. At the gate I was asked if I had a letter giving me permission to record. I didn't. I asked how long it would take to get one and was told three weeks. I asked if I was going to be the first Jew to be turned away from Auschwitz, and they hesitated a minute, then let me through.

Alan said Max went to Germany, too, sometime in the 1970s, to testify against an SS guard. We put him away, Max told Alan when he returned home. If a man is ashamed of his actions in the war, Alan asked me, does he go to a German court to bear witness?

I thought of the way my parents avoided everything to do with the war. They didn't take us to the Holocaust Day commemorations held in survivor communities after the war. Max must have had a very strong constitution to go back to Auschwitz.

Alan said Max didn't drink much, only a whisky or a

beer. He was a big eater, a hungry man. And, like all the survivors I knew, he ate quickly.

He was a snappy dresser. He liked to do things in style. He was generous. But not to me, I thought.

We were nearly at the airport. Alan explained how to tame horses. He told me about the circular paddock, where they can run around and not hurt themselves. He talked about the eye of the trainer, and about the battle of wills between man and horse. When the horse is tired of resisting it puts out its tongue. You have to watch for that: it's a sign that it's ready to negotiate. Then the man can look away from the horse's eyes, glance at his flank or his chest or his neck. But if the struggle is to go on, the trainer looks back into the horse's eyes.

Approach a horse from the side, Alan said, so he can see you have nothing hidden behind your back. Cougars are the natural predators of the horse, and will attack its chest and flanks and belly. Pat a horse on his most sensitive areas and he'll learn to trust you. He is programmed to protect these vulnerabilities. If he gives them up to you, he's yours.

In the plane I looked at the small collection of photographs that Alan had given me. There was the photo of Max taken in 1947. On the back it says *Sierpien*, Polish for August. Just as Alan had described, Max is leaning against a bushy garden wall in rolled-up shirtsleeves, scowling to one side, his left arm crossed over his right, his tattoo displayed and his wedding ring visible. He is handsome and rangy.

There's a front-on headshot, too, from some kind of identification document, but no clue to when and where it was taken.

Another 1947 shot of Max: this time in a long light-coloured trench coat buttoned up to the top, a darker hat on his head, and both hands in his pockets. It's May, spring, and the place is identified as Wiesbaden, the site of one of the Displaced Persons camps where the survivors of the war were gathered by the United Nations Relief and Rehabilitation Administration. This picture was taken by a professional photographer—the stamp and address are on the back.

The last Wiesbaden shot, dated July 1947, must be the one Alan mentioned with Max standing alongside his friend from Greece. They're both in sharp suits, double-breasted, the jackets reaching down to mid-thigh level and the pants wide. Max's suit is of a light colour and he has a flash of white handkerchief in the top pocket, a dark tie and a white shirt. He is holding a pair of wire-rimmed sunglasses. The pants have a sharp crease in them. The men do look like Mafiosi. But maybe they were just survivors who revelled in the possibility of being clean, wearing decent clothes and presenting themselves smartly to the world. We are human beings, they seemed to be saying, and we are ready to start living again.

Then there was a 1956 shot of Max and his wife dancing at a party. Max is in a typically elegant jacket, and there's his white hanky in the top pocket again. His checked tie looks like it's made of silk. His eyes are closed and he has the tiniest smile forming. His wife looks straight into the camera. She's wearing a strappy summer dress and her earrings are clip-on round buttons. She looks like she's enjoying herself. It's taken by another professional photographer, this shot, but this time they are in Melbourne and the photographer is in Alexander Parade, Fitzroy. I turned two in that year.

The last photograph, the only colour one in the batch, is of Alan standing in front of a VW Kombi. Judging by his long sideburns, it must be the early 1970s. He's holding his cousin's daughter, who looks about twelve months old. It's a full-length half-profile shot.

There are two surprising things about this photo. First, Alan is much fuller in the body than the man who just dropped me at the airport. This must have been in his pre-junkie days.

The second thing makes me sit up in my seat as the plane takes off into the serious blue sky, makes me understand why Alan let me have these precious photographs. He has a full head of curly hair, the exact same shade as mine.

8

Good enough for me

FOUR weeks passed before the laboratory called. Their test standard hadn't worked properly and they had to repeat the process. I would have to wait. I have never been good at waiting.

Another four weeks passed before the lab rang again to tell me that Alan's test sample had not been taken correctly and I would have to get another one.

This was odd. I remembered that Alan closed his mouth when he inserted the cotton bud and I couldn't see if it connected with his cheek. I couldn't go up north again, so I got a message to Alan and sent him a new test kit. He was going to have to take this sample without my supervision. I was disappointed and a little suspicious. What exactly did he mean when he told me he never promises anyone anything?

Two months passed and Alan called me back, leaving a message. He had no return number to give me. He was on a horse, he said, because he and his partner were not living together at the moment and she had the car. They had just had another child, a boy. He said that he had taken the new sample about a month ago and sent it down to the laboratory in Sydney. And that he hadn't mentioned anything about me to his mother yet.

It was now about a year since Dad's eightieth birthday: soon we would be gathering again. I had a few more messages from Alan, who was riding around the tropics on a horse and trying to reach me from the occasional phone box he passed. He said that when he was meant to talk to me, he'd get through.

Without warning a letter arrived from the laboratory. I rushed to tear the envelope open. The report inside was titled 'Shared single parent for half-sibship test'. The bottom line read: 'The sibship index = .115 is the ratio of related to unrelated for all the tests. This figure argues against but does not exclude half-sibship.'

Another conversation with the laboratory revealed it was probable that, as Alan's forebears and mine all came from the same small population of Ashkenazi Jews in Poland, there had been quite a bit of inbreeding over the past five hundred years—and that's why it was unclear whether Alan and I were half siblings or just cousins a few times removed. More testing might reveal a clearer answer.

I decided to step back and consider my position. How did I feel? Was I disappointed, or maybe a little relieved?

I wasn't keen to ask for more samples. Alan seemed willing but I sensed distrust below the surface. I couldn't even say whether the latest sample was taken properly. And I didn't think I could travel to Kuranda again so soon, or to wherever Alan's horse had taken him, just to make sure I took it correctly. I had no right to hold Alan down and swab him like a laboratory rat.

But I had to admit there was a sense of relief that I didn't have a firm obligation to the man who was living like an itinerant, his children in a house without walls, his life disrupted. We had a story which seemed to make sense to both of us, but nothing to confirm it.

Perhaps a story was enough. Perhaps I would never know the truth. And perhaps that didn't matter.

It was an old human question, nevertheless: where did I come from? A Yiddish poem by Dovid Hofshteyn, written just after the end of World War I, resonated with me. It begins:

> We spring from rocks
> from rocks ground by millstones of time
> We spring from rocks
> We have tied our fate
> to oceans
> to winds
> to yonder

I printed the poem and stuck it to the wall above my desk.

It's true that we started life on this rock orbiting the sun, and that we are the product of geological time. I thought of the story of Moses striking a rock and turning his staff into a snake. A rock was not a warm and human place to come from, but a rock was at least solid, and in a sense we did spring from it—from dust to dust, as it were. But at this point in my quest it felt second-best to claim general evolution as the explanation for why I was here. I felt illegitimate in some essential way, humiliating myself by knocking on strangers' doors, asking for cell samples and coming up with a result that was inconclusive.

Alan had been kind and welcoming but maybe my visit meant more to him than just a stranger looking for a connection. Maybe he got some credibility from someone outside his circle coming to seek him out. Maybe he thought it might give him clout with his wavering partner. And maybe he was telling me more than I realised when he said he never promised.

I remembered the way he approached me in the Cairns airport, the first time I met him: coming up alongside me. I remembered the conversation about how to gain the confidence of a strange horse. *Approach a horse from the side so he can see you've got nothing hiding behind your back.*

I felt as if I'd been managed by an excellent horse whisperer—another survivor, in his own way. Perhaps, despite welcoming me, he didn't want me to find a solid link with Max. How could he trust me?

But I had come for a story and I had left with a story and such was its power that I refused to give up on it.

It was Dad's eighty-first birthday and the family was about to reassemble—except for my younger daughter, who was still in Jerusalem. There was the usual silent ghost, too: Mama. I was beginning to question the impression I'd always had of her, thinking of the subterfuge she had carried off.

I cooked a big pasta sauce while listening to Aretha Franklin singing 'Respect'. I always got nervous before Dad was due to arrive, so my elder daughter and I shared a joint in the back garden. She'd rolled it with mint tea—it was meant to be healthier, she said. By the time we sat down at the table with Dad the effect was kicking in, and my daughter and I began to giggle.

Dad said he'd like some wine and I passed him the bottle. He poured himself a glass, then topped up the glasses of my twelve-year-old nephew and his seven-year-old brother. I found myself laughing uncontrollably at the end of the table, remembering the way my quest had begun a year earlier.

'I don't want my children drinking wine, Dad,' my sister said.

'But they asked for it and I gave it to them,' he said defensively.

My head was in my hands, and I was thinking that I should have started smoking mint tea years ago.

Later, I found a note in my pocket that Dad had passed me across the table.

> The last book of Isaac Bashevis Singer—Printed 1999
> 'The Shadows of the Hutson'
> We can all know everythink, each one learn
> his own leson. Knowledge can never come only
> to a simple individual it grows out of experience
> of the whole human species.

Then, a few days later, he sent me a letter:

> Dear Ramona,
> Thanks you very much for making for me the Birthday, with cakes and candles. It took me 45 years for it. I like the party but did not like your whispering to your sister's ear.

We have to meet again at your sister's or in my
place for a brunch, only you organise when it going
to be comfortable and just ring me. Thanks again
for the party and present.
Dad

Enclosed was a twenty-dollar note for my daughter in Israel.

Why was every small interaction with him so fraught?
Why did he send money for one of my daughters and not for
the other? This was a pattern established years ago: picking
out one child for attention. The children were beyond
offence; they saw it as a quirk. I was still ready to be stung.

I checked the reference in the note. The book he'd
mentioned was indeed the last by Singer, who died in 1991.
Shadows on the Hudson was translated from Yiddish to English
and finally published in 1998. Dad hadn't read more than
Time magazine for years, as far as I knew—but what did I
really know about him? This was only one of many occasions
when he would hand me a gnomic note or an article torn
from a magazine without explanation.

Was the quote from the book or from a review of the book
in *Time*? Did it have anything to do with my search for the
truth, or was it merely something that had appealed to him?

And the letter. What did he mean about my whispering
with my sister? I was whispering with my daughter. Was he
confused, or was I?

Two months later, after he'd left seven messages on my
answering machine, I finally spoke to Alan. He was calling

from a phone box, having come in to town to do his washing. He and his partner had finally split up, and his daughter stayed with him two days a week. His baby son was fine, he said. He sounded all right, although he admitted that things had been hard.

I explained again the results of the DNA tests. He said he would be my spiritual brother if nothing else. I was ashamed of my reticence, embarrassed at having bowled into his life with an outlandish story that now seemed to be unprovable. I thanked him for his kindness in accepting me and going through the testing process.

He said he didn't mind. That it was interesting. That my voice was up at his place where he listened to me on the radio. And that he and his mates always read my columns in the newspapers.

See you, darling, he whispered, as we said goodbye.

When his younger cousin called, I told him the results of the DNA test. 'If it was a murder trial, you wouldn't get a conviction,' he said. 'But since it's a cousin trial, it's good enough for me.'

The year rolled by. A month before Dad's next birthday my sister called me and then arrived on my doorstep with my oldest nephew. He was thirteen now, a young man. He had finished *The Lord of the Rings* and wanted me to buy him another Tolkien book. Our relationship was founded on a love of books and learning new languages.

I took him to the bookshop where I had an account. He was almost too shy to ask for the book he wanted. I saw him blushing at the thought of going up to the counter, and later he was too embarrassed to get a straw for his milkshake. I had forgotten how painful that age can be, when you think everyone is looking at you, judging every action.

I looked at my nephew's eyes and his fair skin, and I was sad that I couldn't say for sure that he shared these features with me. Now there was the possibility that these things came from my real father, the one who couldn't be his mother's father.

Yet I felt that my sister and I were closer since this story began evolving. Both of us were somewhat adrift and trying to comfort each other. I saw her anew. I saw she had our mother's hips and legs and narrow shoulders. And smaller stature: I towered over her. Whose shoulders did I have?

I have a photograph of Mama holding me as a baby on St Kilda Beach. Who was holding the camera? I suddenly remembered that she'd told me that Mr Lederman took lots of photos of me—on the potty, for example. So he must have known her when I was a baby. I recalled his claim that he may have met her afterwards, and thought again that he was a liar and a coward. Or maybe she was the liar, and the one who was holding the camera was Max.

There she was in the black-and-white snap with bevelled edges, twenty-seven going on twenty-eight, proud of what she had produced. I tried to be angry with her for messing things up so profoundly, but I couldn't find it in my heart to sustain the feeling. I was sorry for her and admired her pluck: to have a child who was not her husband's issue and to get away with it. I saw a news report about ten per cent of paternity tests giving negative results. Mama was not alone.

In the shower I washed my hair and imagined taking a few hairs from Dad's head while he was still alive, and waiting till he had died to match them to my sister and me. I thought about trying to get a sample unobtrusively. We could lie and say that one of my sister's kids had an iron deficiency and that the whole family had to have our hair tested for genetic transmission. This would be unethical. But if we held back the testing until he was dead, and then took a sample (from his dead body? his hairbrush? how would I get access to that? what was I thinking?), maybe that would be more ethical.

We shouldn't have to live with this uncertainty all of our lives, I thought. We weren't at fault—didn't we have a right to know the answers to these questions? But why was I saying 'we' when I seemed to be the only person troubled by them?

A friend invited me to a Sabbath meal at a young rabbi's home. His wife was pregnant with their eighth child. The seven children sat quietly waiting for their mother to finish clearing the table. There was no arguing, no restlessness. The rabbi asked the children if they had anything to show him. They slipped off their chairs and surrounded him, holding pictures they had drawn, stories they had written, things they had made. He let the youngest girl, about three years old, climb onto his knee. I ached to be the youngest one, to plant myself on his lap and lean my back against his belly.

When I drove home the men on the street who caught my eyes were the older ones, the greyer ones. If I had to ask a trusted older man for advice, to whom would I go? What would I want to be told? Only that I was a good girl, a clever girl; that he'd look after me, was proud of me and loved me, and that one day another man would love me, too.

Throughout this time I had been making notes about who I'd met and what I'd found. It was odd to be keeping a secret diary, morbid to be waiting for Dad to die. I wondered if I would grieve for him. I had a sense I'd be sad for everything he didn't have and everything I didn't have, and for the world that had made his live so difficult and my life with him so confused.

I imagined myself at Dad's funeral, not being able to cry, not being able to seem bereft in front of others, their judgements clear. Maybe my sister and I would laugh, as we often do when we're hysterical. We cackled uncontrollably when Mama was in her final coma. She'd been taken unconscious from her bed at our home to a small hospital nearby, and died there three days later.

I had felt like an orphan. Dad didn't see me for months—not until he visited the hospital when I had my second daughter. He didn't mention Mama's death and only stayed for a few minutes. The father I had couldn't look after me. Nor did he take an interest in me. Everything seemed to be too much trouble for him. He was always tired, or trying to make sure he was the centre of attention. He hated the competition of children.

At my niece's school play a few weeks after his latest birthday, Dad stood up at the end during the applause, as if they were showering him with appreciation. He bowed from the front row. Looking back now, I suspect this must have been a sign of growing dementia, but it was intriguing to see his behaviour become more obvious, rather than being masked as before.

In the new year I had dinner with my sister. As we were walking back to her car we bumped into a friend of hers from high school, a woman I knew too, sitting with her family out the front of a restaurant.

Her husband was next to their nine-year-old daughter, and it was hard to take my eyes from the loving scene. Father and daughter chatted about what music she wanted to buy and what food she wanted to order. He stroked her hair and she leaned on him. When she said she was cold, he gave her his jumper.

My sister talked to her friend about all the things that had happened in the past year. And then she said, 'Oh, and yes, we found out something else. Perhaps you should tell this, Ramona?'

But I was interested to hear how she would tell it, what she would say.

She said that I had made enormous efforts and had found out that we were half-sisters, and that neither of us knew who our biological father was. She joked that she had had enough to deal with that year but that I had needed to follow the story and so she had been dragged along.

Her friend asked if it was like being in the sidecar of a motorbike I was driving. My sister agreed enthusiastically.

I thought of my secret diary. I was a writer, and writers want to write books. I wanted to tell people what I had been thinking about. How was I going to bring along others in my family on this part of my journey: how many sidecars was I attaching to this motorbike of mine?

I asked my younger daughter about the implications of my quest in the religious or Halakhic sense. She responded in the true spirit of the rabbis. If my sister and I didn't know for sure who our fathers were, then maybe Dad was our father.

But, I said, he can only be the father of one of us. So one of us is a bastard. And that bastard has broken Halakhic law by marrying a person who is not a bastard, instead of finding another bastard to marry. For ten generations, or possibly until the end of time. According to this law, either she and her sister or their cousins are bastards. I had to remind her, and myself, that I didn't accept these rules.

I entertained the thought of writing the story into a novel that could take the weight of truth. But I kept coming up against the obvious logical conundrum. How could a story about hidden truths, shame and disgrace, secrets and lies, be told anything less than truthfully after all these years?

9

Who likes funerals?

DESPITE the lack of unequivocal genetic evidence about my connection to Max, I was not ready to forsake him. I especially liked the story of the tattooed number on his arm—the way he thought about it marking his survival.

I'd found an account by Mayer Abramowitz, an American army rabbi serving in the Schlachtensee Displaced Persons' Camp in Germany—where Mama and Dad spent time after the war—of a young woman who was dismissed from her job. She was a waitress in a dining room for military personnel at the nearby airbase. He described being absorbed by the 'bluish green number, written in large, upper case lettering, stretching along her forearm...I couldn't look away from the tattoo. I couldn't look at her face. Do I ask about the number? Do I act normally as though it wasn't there?' He was reminded of the time he saw a farmer brand a cow. The reason given for the woman's dismissal was that the staff and the military men who ate there were disturbed by her tattoo. She was reinstated after Abramowitz intervened.

Like this woman's, Max's tattoo was in large digits on

the top of his forearm rather than the smaller ones I'd seen, often on the inner arm. I wrote to Dr Stephen Feinstein at the Center for Holocaust and Genocide Studies at the University of Minnesota, asking him about this discrepancy. He explained that there seemed to have been a general pattern of placing the tattoo so that it could be read when the inmate held the arm across the chest—to the eye of the bearer it was usually upside down. He said that size varied. One woman he met whose numbers were at least two inches high told him that she'd had an encounter with some skinhead types in an American mall who were impressed with it and 'wanted to know where she had it done'.

In camp slang, Feinstein said, the tattoo was a 'cremation number'—Auschwitz was part of the Third Reich and all deaths theoretically required a death certificate. But I knew that only those selected for work were tattooed. Those slated for immediate death did not have ink wasted on them.

Still, the 'cremation number' was new to me. Shame would turn to pride, surely, if you could look down at your arm and see that you had outwitted death.

Dad had turned eighty-two and we'd gathered at his place for lunch. My older daughter was at a ten-day silent retreat in the Blue Mountains. I could think of nothing worse. Even being here at this table was better than ten days without speaking.

My younger daughter had brought her new boyfriend, who was eagerly asking Dad about his life. I was impressed with his enthusiasm and politeness but my sister and I rolled our eyes when we heard Dad telling familiar anecdotes, punctuated with his theatrical sighs.

As we were leaving, Dad approached me with a copy of *Time* magazine in his hand. He gripped my forearm with his other hand and said, 'You always wanted Utopia, but read this story on page fifty-six. It doesn't exist!' I said it was a shocking way to break the news to me and rushed to tell my sister.

Two months later we were angry with him again. He didn't show up to the funeral of my sister's father-in-law or to any of the *minyans*, the week of evening prayer gatherings after it, because, he said, he didn't like funerals. I asked him: But who likes funerals? He didn't like her father-in-law either, because he'd stopped Dad from bringing his second wife to my sister's wedding. Okay—but we thought Dad could have made the effort for my sister's sake.

We remembered how he avoided us after Mama's death, and never asked how it was for us to have our mother die after we'd looked after her by ourselves, with no help from anyone. How could he really be our father when he never behaved like a father should do?

He did call us a few weeks after Mama's funeral—to say that he'd put a caveat on her estate, so that we couldn't sell it without the opportunity for him to claim an interest. They'd already divorced and split their finances fifty-fifty by then: more than fair, as my mother was too sick to work and my sister was still a student living at home.

His callousness was shocking to me, as was his disregard for the needs of my sister and for our distress so soon after our mother had died. We assumed that his new circumstances dictated his actions. It explained some of the exasperation I felt when dealing with Dad in the years afterwards, and my inability to cut him some slack.

When I returned from a dog-sledding trip to Canada with a deep-vein thrombosis in my leg, which meant I was relegated to the couch for rest, he called to say he was sending me smoked salmon in the post because it upset him to see sickness. He didn't like dead people or funerals and now he didn't like sick people either, even one who was supposed to be his daughter.

I had a restless night's sleep thinking about what he'd said, then called him back to say that sending me smoked salmon in the mail was the most idiotic thing I'd ever heard of and that he shouldn't do it. But I've organised my whole day around it, he said, disappointed.

It wasn't a good week. A now elderly woman I'd paid to help me with child care after my mother died, my marriage ended and my sister left home called to warn me that she had met my first informant, my primary witness, Bern, at a church meeting, and that she seemed emotionally troubled. I was concerned to hear this and worried that I might be following a false lead in my search, until the church source herself proved to be confused and unstable. Was her report just a fantasy? Why did I have to question the reliability of my most important sources? Was it them or was it me? I was feeling a little crazy myself.

That year I was particularly sensitive to things that made me feel like an outsider. I had taken the idea of being a *mamzer* to heart. I felt passed over at Passover when I was not invited to my sister's family Seder at her mother-in-law's home. Instead, she invited me to the second night at her house, which has always been considered (by me, at least) to be the second-class Seder. The first night is full of enthusiastic singing and eating matzo-ball soup and the rest of the feasting and reading from the *Haggadah* the liberation story of the flight from Egyptian slavery. The second night is for the also-rans and for leftover food from the first night's festivities.

I would have nowhere to go on the first night, as my children were spoken for at their father's house, and I imagined a cold, lonely night of watching TV and feeling rejected. It was a bit ridiculous to be afraid of the cold. I had central heating, and an open fireplace and wood piled up at the back door.

Max's younger nephew had invited me to their first-night Seder, an invitation I declined after a bit of toing and froing. It was kind of them, but some of those present would have known about our story and others wouldn't, including the man who might well be my uncle. I was unhappy about coming to the table as a stranger and a cause of shame.

Deeply ambivalent about being in the second rank at my sister's place, I nevertheless dutifully made a cake and the sweet *charoset*, a mixture of nuts and apple and honey to symbolise the mortar of the Egyptian pyramids built by Jewish slaves. I set off into the night to her house.

A few weeks later, at a performance of *Julius Caesar*, I met Max's younger nephew in the foyer. I introduced him as my cousin to my friend, and she said she saw the family resemblance in his eyes. He said that it was good that I hadn't come to Passover as his father, who was ninety-two, had collapsed and been taken to hospital in an ambulance. The night had been cut short.

The old man had later recovered. Still, I was relieved not to have been the cause of his collapse and imagined the scene if I had found it too hard not to pump him for stories, which might have seemed the reason for his turn. At least *this* wasn't my fault.

By this stage I'd decided to end the psychoanalysis I'd been having for four and a half years. I thought that I had made some progress in understanding myself and perhaps even why my life had taken the turns it had. My analyst was Austrian, formal and clever; we had explored my quest for the truth about my father; and although I found the sessions intriguing and rewarding, if gruelling, I could no longer afford to spend time and money on the couch. I needed to pursue my enquiries outside that small room.

At the final appointment I shook my analyst's hand and thanked him. He smiled and said it had been his pleasure. As I made my way down his staircase for the last time, I breathed a sigh of relief and accomplishment.

Ending analysis gave me back my time. No longer did I have to make sure I was available three mornings a week. I'd finally worked long enough to take long-service leave and had been awarded a travelling fellowship by the Goethe-Institut to spend two months in Berlin learning German, meeting arts and literary figures, and researching a film script that I wanted to write.

I rang Dad to say I would have to miss his eighty-third birthday that year, and to tell him the good news. He had good news, too. A letter had arrived explaining that the German government was paying him a few thousand dollars in compensation for being a slave labourer in Poland under the Third Reich. So now we both had German scholarships.

It was thirty years since I'd sat in a language class like this one in Berlin, waiting for the teacher to begin. We were from all over the world—Japan, Korea, Sweden, Uzbekistan, Croatia, Israel and the USA—and I was from the most exotic place anyone could think of, Australia, at the bottom of the globe. Our lingua franca would be the German that none of us could yet speak.

The little Japanese woman had a porcelain face and a squeaky voice. The young man from Korea was formal and inscrutable. The woman from Uzbekistan was quiet, with warm eyes. The Croatian was serious, the Swedish boy was shy, the Israeli was casual and the American chewed gum.

By the end of the first class we could say our names, our homelands, our jobs. The Japanese girl was studying singing, the Korean had his own orchestra and played the double bass, and the Uzbekistani woman was a theatre director. The Croatian was into multimedia, the American was a painter, the Israeli a social worker with parents from Ukraine.

By the end of the first week we were relieved to be standing in the courtyard—in the break from the four-and-a-half-hour class—speaking snatches of English to those who could understand, and hearing Spanish, French, Greek, Russian and other languages. What a relief it was to be speaking a language you'd mastered—how excruciating to have lost the instrument of your self-presentation, which you were used to using with pride.

Back in the class Herr P. from Korea had shown just how versatile he was, having developed a sophisticated form of sign language in which he used his whole body to convey meaning. Fraulein O. from Japan hardly spoke, but I noticed that each day her homework was returned with hardly a correction, while mine was a mess of red lines. Herr M. from Croatia was a teacher himself, and had worked out interesting ways to remember things, trying out all the grammatical forms as soon as he had heard them.

Each day I understood a little more of what people were saying to each other on the U-Bahn. The advertising and information signs in the street began to make sense. It was like putting on a pair of corrective spectacles and having the blur come into focus.

We performed little plays—in the shop, at the doctor's surgery, buying furniture—and Frau A. from Uzbekistan delighted us with her performances and those of her group, which she directed with glee. Herr P. from Korea was a joker, and began many of his interventions with the phrase 'in Korea': we learned to wait for the phrase and laugh with him. Somehow we talked Fraulein O. from Japan into singing for us and she astounded us all with her favourite German *Lied*: Schubert's 'Die Forelle', The Trout. From her slight frame emanated a wonderful voice, clear and strong.

My approach to learning languages was to cast off shore, regardless of the niceties of grammar. I said what I wanted to say in a mixture of ungrammatical German and the Yiddish of my family home, which was itself a sixteenth-century

German dialect with snatches of Hebrew and Slavic words thrown into the mix. My teacher was no doubt intrigued (it must have been like hearing an Appalachian dialect at a New York party) but she gently corrected me at every turn.

We were asked to give a short talk in German about our countries. Fraulein O. told us of a mysterious lake which is usually covered with fog, and an ancient belief about young women who see the lake. Either they must see the lake in order to marry or else if they see the lake they will never marry. We were confused. Herrs USA (an especially hesitant speaker of German), Croatia and Korea took turns to draw pictures on the whiteboard—of a lake, a woman, a man—and perform actions. Fraulein O. shook her head at each bad German interpretation. At last the teacher clarified the problem, revealing that she not only spoke excellent English but perfect Japanese, too.

We began to meet outside the class. Herr P. from Korea was an expert at getting cheap opera and concert tickets, and we went together in the evenings. Frau A. from Uzbekistan gave us theatre tips, telling us what to see. When one of us travelled to give a concert or a lecture, or to a conference, the others were full of questions afterwards. We stayed in class during the break, or went together to buy cheese rolls and speak German in the street. We laughed at each other's mistakes in pronunciation, they told me I asked too many questions because I was a journalist, and we exclaimed with delight when someone got a good mark on a test.

Near the end of eight weeks we were astounded when Herr USA gave a talk about a German techno group. He was fluent, and introduced us to many new words. We suspected he had found himself a German lover, but he insisted that he had just been doing his homework.

The subtleties and talents of each person, their character, history and experience, were revealed as the layers of unfamiliarity were stripped away. Our new shared language allowed us to marvel at the Korean habit of sleeping on the floor and bringing rice tea to anyone with a cold. We saw the Croatian's wedding photographs: a serious young couple observing the Catholic rite. The Israeli gave us her passionate views about the Berlin Jewish Museum exhibition, and the Swedish boy offered insightful comments about his country's welfare system.

In my talk about Australia I found myself describing a vast country with three time zones and many strange animals, just as a child might do. I told them about the Rainbow Serpent at Uluru, *die Regenbogenschlange*, and they seemed impressed—although I'm not sure they understood that it was a mythical beast. They thought I was very brave for surviving in Australia, with its snakes and sharks and hungry crocodiles, and this made me oddly proud.

We were sad to leave each other after our time together, and passed around addresses and promised to meet in Tashkent or Kyoto or on some far-flung border. Our language adventure had been a lesson in humility, in tolerance and in the joys of learning. We took ourselves off into the city, to see what lay ahead.

Each afternoon after class I'd made my way back to the flat where I was billeted, to do my homework. There I was supervised by the Polish cleaning lady, who tried to help me. I could smell alcohol on her breath, and I suspected that she didn't know much more German than I did, especially when some of the red-lined corrections on my work were to the suggestions she had made forcefully over my shoulder.

I studied the German faces in the trains and one day sat opposite two men, brothers I assumed, who looked like elves. They were short; their eyes were close together; they had large ears that sat low on their heads, and long wispy hair. One wore a wedding ring. They were both in trousers that were too short for them. They sat very close together. My gaze kept returning to them, so much did they look like illustrations from a story by the Brothers Grimm. I thought I could see tufts of hair growing out of their ears, but it was difficult from my angled view to say for sure.

Later that day I searched for the old synagogue just off Kurfürstendamm, which is hard to spot. I was looking for a Star of David and by chance saw a notice for a Yiddish play in the window of a bookshop. A policeman showed me the entrance to what looked like an apartment building. When I went through the gates I was met by a couple of swarthy Israeli guards who said that the Orthodox synagogue wasn't open for tourists. But I'm Jewish, I said, and I'm not a tourist. They asked me where I was from and searched my bag.

The synagogue was across the open courtyard. I found the women's section at the back of a large domed cupola, its plaster curlicues painted in green and red and white. The congregation seemed very old, very Russian. None of the women spoke to me.

I became self-conscious and made my way back to the

courtyard, where I took out my map of the U-Bahn to plan the next part of my day. A man in his sixties came over and asked in German how long I would be in Berlin. I told him, in my self-styled Yiddish-German way, where I was from and what I was doing here.

He asked if I wanted to see the ritual bath, the *mikveh*, and I said no, I didn't need it. He didn't need it either, he said. And that I was beautiful and his wife had died some years back and I should come home with him and he would give me food and something to drink.

It was hard to be gracious in a language you have almost no command over, but I said not today. They had another service later that night, he replied, and he would wait for me.

The man was like a character from an Isaac Bashevis Singer story. He came very close to me and asked my name. When I told him he whispered it, stood on his tiptoes and kissed me on the cheek.

I think you are so beautiful, he said. Come home with me. I am from Uzbekistan and we have such hot blood there. Do you understand what I mean? It is good for a man to have hot blood.

I said I didn't understand, that I was fluent only in English.

I could come to his house and teach him English, he said—he already spoke fifteen other languages. Uzbeki-stani, Ukrainian, Arabic, Polish, German, Hebrew...Another man interrupted then, and asked him to fetch something from the storage cupboard.

He was the caretaker of the synagogue, I realised, and as he crossed the courtyard towards the other man he said: Don't forget, Ramona—I'll be waiting for you tonight, Ramona, Ramona, Ramona.

That night I was joining a friend from the Goethe-Institut to hear a famous baritone perform at the Berlin Philharmoniker. The building is designed like a ship, with the orchestra deep in the hold and the audience surrounding the stage, looking down. We were high in the gods on the fifth level, first hearing Webern cantatas, then the singer we were waiting for. He came on for some Mahler *Lieder*. I knew nothing about him, so it was a surprise to see a man affected by Thalidomide, with flipper hands which emerged from his shoulders, and stunted legs.

As soon as they saw him the audience applauded wildly. He sang well, and they clapped and clapped; he shook hands with the conductor and the first violinist; and the audience would only let him leave the stage after six bows.

All I could think of was that sixty years earlier they would have gassed him, and now they hailed him. It was as if he was their pet monster, *homunculus extraordinaire*.

The man sitting next to me was with his ancient mother, who was in a wheelchair. She was severe, and kept insisting he get things for her—her shawl, a program, her lunettes. When I returned to my seat at the end of the inter-mission I saw her up and pushing her wheelchair, stagger-ing behind it, wraithlike yet determined. 'Mama, Mama!' the man said. 'I can't leave you for two minutes.' But she had wanted something and wanted it right away.

When we sat down again the orchestra began playing Wagner, and the man and his mother adored it. The music was beautiful—the whole orchestra swayed. Wagner reminded me of the history of hatred in this city, and the old woman was now beating perfect time with the orchestra, her arthritic fingers tapping on her armrest. She let out small noises of approval and her son nodded.

I found her chilling, and imagined that she had been a proud Nazi in years gone by. In the three months I was away I was treated well by my hosts and made friends with the woman with whom I was billeted, and I didn't think about Dad much at all. But I was constantly aware of being a stranger, of being from a group that had been despised in these streets not so long ago, constantly aware of where I had come from and how the people around me might view me if they knew who I really was.

But who was I, really?

Dad was now eighty-four. I could hear a slight slurring on the phone when I called him to tell him about my younger daughter's new job. He told me he was having trouble with his tear ducts, which meant he couldn't stop crying and he would get highly emotional. I wondered how much more emotional he could possibly be, as I had always found him on the verge of hysteria.

But he was still dancing. Every Saturday night he and his wife went to the German Club near my house. I could never understand why a Holocaust survivor wanted to spend his Saturday nights with Germans. Though what did I know about his whims and wishes? His second wife had been born into a Christian family in Germany and her first husband had been Jewish, too. Maybe Dad enjoyed having

Germans serve him. He said that once the music started up at the club he 'danced non-stop for the whole night'.

He was particularly upset this day because one of his card-playing friends had rung him to say that he had pancreatic cancer and was going to die. Dad told me that he'd replied: 'Why did you tell me this? Don't you know how emotional I get?' Then he hung up on his friend.

But Dad, I said, it isn't you who has the cancer—it's him.

'But why did he tell me?'

It's a privilege, I said, to be the one who is told.

'But I can't stand the emotion when a friend of mine dies.'

I suggested he play cards with younger people.

'Someone said I should go to a psychiatrist,' he said.

I told him that I thought it was a good idea. That I had done so and it did me a lot of good.

'Really?' he said. 'Then perhaps I will.'

He had stopped driving recently, after he ploughed his new car into a parked vehicle.

'I'm getting old,' he said, his voice thickening in my ear.

I thought he might have a stroke, and silently I wished him a massive one, a final one, right there on the dance floor in full flight before the assembled Germans.

Shortly after this conversation, his dancing came to a halt. He went to hospital with heart failure, which may have been what I heard in the thickening of his tongue on the phone, but my sister said his GP had told her that Dad had kidney and liver failure, and that he'd been drinking heavily.

Maybe he had been drunk when we spoke. I was never good at working out if people were drinkers. I once had a long-distance relationship with someone whose obvious alcoholism was hard for me to diagnose even with the starkest of clues, like piles of empty bottles stacked up in his shed, and bruises and cuts on his forehead where he had landed face down on his brick floor after a long night's secret drinking.

I called Dad in hospital several times but he was hard to engage with and insisted he didn't want to be visited. My sister took over monitoring him by phone. My older daughter made a few doctorly calls. According to my sister, Dad's wife and stepdaughter had given their views to the hospital about what his treatment plan should be if his condition worsened.

I was relieved that it was not going to be up to me to decide if he should be treated or when treatment should be withdrawn. He was an often confused, unhappy, unhealthy old man. Those who were close to him should decide.

I felt like he was an old friend of the family, not my father, that I was not in the position of the daughter who was obliged to do something. My sister was taking responsibility, and I hoped this was a role she was more comfortable in playing than I would be. I had taken responsibility for Mama when she was dying, as my sister was four years younger and had just started university. And maybe she genuinely thought Dad was her father—though I'd never seen him show her any real care or understanding either.

I was relieved of duty. In truth, I relieved myself of duty.

On the phone a few days later Dad said, 'The main thing in life is to be friendly.' He was sharing a room with a man whom he described as blind, deaf and mute. He reported that the man's family laughed at Dad's jokes and were amazed that he was the same age as their poor benighted relative. He assumed they were delighted by him, preferring him to their own kin.

I noted that although he didn't want us to visit he was eagerly expecting his stepson-in-law at any moment. Obviously he felt more comfortable with his new family, and who could blame him? I was glad to just make phone calls and not to have his care on my conscience. Perhaps this was the best evidence yet that we were not related. Could I have such sangfroid if I thought that I was losing my dear old father?

10

The pregnant boy
of Kazakhstan

BY the time of his eighty-fifth birthday, Dad had been out of
hospital for several months. I called to ask him where he'd
like to go to celebrate. Same place, he said, according to his
wife, who now answered all their phone calls. I imagined
the food being served on forklift trucks.

This time my older daughter would be studying at
Berkeley, in California, with her new husband. My younger
daughter was coming with her fiancé, who would not be
eating, as this wasn't a kosher restaurant.

Dad's wife said that he had slowed down and wasn't
walking around the neighbourhood anymore, though he
was still reading. He was in bed by nine-thirty each night.
Ah, what can you expect when you get old, she said. That's
my bedtime, too, I thought.

I asked her if she was coping, hoping she would say yes
and that I wouldn't have to offer to do anything for them. I
volunteered to ring my sister and daughter to tell them the
date of the lunch. This was in lieu of doing anything really

helpful, for which I could not muster the enthusiasm.

My sister was indignant when I called, partly because it was only 8 a.m. on a work day and partly because Dad hadn't invited her himself. Everyone in this family hated being overlooked, even by people to whom they were not necessarily related. I had to tell her that I'd suggested the party and that I hadn't even spoken to Dad, only to his wife.

When people asked about my father—if I had one, if I saw him much—I was at a loss for words. I called him sometimes but he could hardly hear me, as he refused to wear his hearing aid. He told me, over and over again, stories about how other people had failed him, about how hard it was to get old.

I didn't feel guilty about this. I didn't feel anything much. I had little emotional connection with Dad, except in an abstract way.

Now I thought of him as an old man, a survivor. A man who had somehow persuaded his wife to look after him for all the years since he'd left my mother. He must have made her happy, at least for a while, and I felt she deserved every cent of the meagre estate he would leave when he died.

Please, God, I prayed sometimes, *if you are there, make her outlast him.*

Every time I went away for work I imagined he would die and I would be summoned to the funeral but, because of the Jewish rules of a quick burial, I wouldn't be able to make it in time and so my sister and the rest of the family would have to shoulder the burden alone. I was refusing, in my imagination, to take on the role of the eldest child—after all, I had never felt entitled to anything from him.

I hadn't asked him for money since he declined to pay sixty dollars in union fees for my first year of university. Even though I had won a scholarship, he was worried that a university education would spoil my chances of marriage. Like Mama, I would read too many books—in his opinion, that was always the problem with her.

I never asked him for help of any kind, through the hardship of bringing up my kids alone and the scrapes I got myself into with disappointing love affairs, and it was never forthcoming. Why then, I thought, should I put myself out, except to behave in a decent way, the way you might for a neighbour or an old retainer?

What kind of an old retainer was he, anyway? What did he do for me that you might pay someone to do?

I was ashamed of thinking like this; it was very bad. Dad had supported me when I was a child, through his work at the factory, and later at the shop, and then at the factory again. But then, he was supposed to be my father. Surely he got kudos for having two girls who were good at school and who went to university on scholarships and got married and had children? That was what we were supposed to do. And now I had set him adrift, the man for whom I felt no love, the man who shared our house for all those years, the man with whom I shared no understanding and no deep connection. I had, I reasoned, been passed over, and so I could set myself free.

Later, Dad called to invite me to the lunch I had organised for him. He had called my sister, too, and told her that the gift we gave him the year before was a 'terrible, stupid present'.

We'd banded together and bought him and his wife season passes to the cinema near their home. 'I haven't even used one of the tickets,' he told my sister.

We were hurt. I thought it was a good present, she said. It *was* a good present, I said. It was a typical response from him. Nothing was ever right: we were never right, he was never right, we were a mismatch.

I thought of my ridiculous trip to Poland to research my roots and the time I spent in Siedlce, his hometown, which was pointless now, except for having found Mama and Dad's incomplete marriage certificate. The certificate was not the only thing incomplete about their marriage. Even the remnants they left behind were disintegrating.

I restarted my quest on a different tack, researching a new part of Poland, Max Dunne's hometown of Mława. Online I found a memoir written by Dr Izhak Ze'ev Yunis from Tel Aviv. It was dated 1949 and called 'The Old Hometown'. I started by searching for Max's birth surname, Adunaj, but none of the memories of rabbis and butchers and leather workers and mad grocers' wives mentioned anyone by that name.

Next I looked at the records held in Salt Lake City, Utah. Between 1968 and 1992 Mormons microfilmed more than two thousand reels of nineteenth-century Jewish records from the Polish State Archives. It was something to do with their interests in reverse-baptising people—that is, baptising dead people as Mormons. Regardless of whether my dead relatives were now officially Mormons, or were indeed my relatives, I was pleased to see the energy with which these people had pursued the collection of names in far-flung places. There were Adunajs listed in the records, and it felt slightly pathetic to be sidling up to yet another lot of strangers, this time dead ones, in an attempt to be tied in some way to the town of Mława. Not long before I'd been ready to throw my lot in with Siedlce. Any port in a storm—a storm of my own making.

This disturbing inclination to latch on to each possible familial connection drew me to media stories of mysterious parenthood and family secrets. I read about a man who sought the return of seventy-five thousand dollars in school fees and support payments after he discovered that he was not the biological father of his ex-wife's child. He'd become suspicious when he and his new partner had trouble conceiving: he must have found out then that he was sterile. He still loved the child he'd raised with his ex-wife, he said, and still wanted visiting rights. The judge said there could be no rights without responsibilities. I thought again of the time—almost a decade—that Dad and Mama spent trying to have children before I came along.

Dad wrote to me once after I questioned him about their relationship:

I never did finish the story because you are always in a hurry. I told you how I met your Mother and she stayed with me. It is impossible to describe the loneliness we had losing all our family in one day. The families in Poland were much closer than here. You can imagine when you lose one member of a family it's a tragedy and that we lost both our families—this closeness drew us more and more together. You seek in that single person

your brother, sister, mother, everything. I fell in love with her because it was my first love. I cannot recall up to the war and of course in the war I never had a girl for sex, she was all for me. After a short time we start to talk about marriage. I did know a girl before the war, Hanka Białastocka, she wanted me because I was the secretary from Siedlce and had the list of fifty-one survivors from the fourteen thousand Jews before the war. Later when the war finished she came back from Russia where some had survived. I was already hooked up with Mum so I went to the market and bought a piece of new material made of paper mixed with cotton and made myself a suit and for her I bought a piece of pink material with little white flowers and I made a simple wedding frock. This was the first Jewish wedding in the town after the war and all the survivors came, everybody bought some sort of food and there was no rabbi, only a man who knew how to write the *ksuba*, the marriage contract...This ends this story, some other time I will write to you how I wanted to have you and waited for nine years before I got you and this was the happiest day of my life when you were born.
Thank you,
Dad

Framing my birth as the culmination of their having risen, phoenix-like, from the ashes of Nazi Europe gave context to many of my parents' actions. Mama had talked about how desperate Dad had been to have a child, about how for him success depended on building a family. She said that they fought whenever she got her period. Maybe her going outside the marriage stemmed from a desire to give him what he wanted, perhaps what she wanted, too? Not so much out of love for him, but out of a need to keep things at home peaceful? It's only in fairytales that people do things for one reason. Real life is far more complex.

Despite the touching letter, I felt sure that Dad's sense of his responsibility for me and my sister ended when he left our house, all those years ago, to take up with a new woman. I was less certain about where my responsibilities to him began and ended.

And there were other relationships to analyse. My sister told me she had explained our story so far to her daughter, who recognised that it was sad and pointed out that she had never felt close to Dad. She then tried to work out whose father he was.

To my relief, she told her mother that she didn't feel any differently about me. In my rush to investigate my hunches, my need to know had been so great that I had not thought about the effect that half-siblingship might have on my relationships with my sister's children. I loved them fiercely, and I couldn't imagine feeling closer to them. My sister was right: anything I needed to know and anything I uncovered directly affected others.

Dad's eighty-fifth birthday arrived, and this time there were fewer people eating Sunday lunch at the same old restaurant. There must have been new owners, because the menu seemed a little changed—but the food still came piled on massive plates. This time Dad hadn't done the ordering and he was not insisting on paying, as he usually did, so my sister and I split the bill. The children were at one end of the table; they had exams that week or had been up all night at parties—I noticed that my older nephew, who was not yet a teenager at Dad's eightieth birthday, now noticeably needed a shave.

Dad had been ill, but he'd picked up again, according to his wife. He'd given up playing cards three nights a week. He said he was happy not to be seeing the men he'd played with for fifteen years. Why, I asked, didn't he play during the day? His wife said that was when he had his nap. All day? But they had to go to the coffee shop in the mornings. Their days were precisely organised and the timetable unwavering.

When I arrived at the restaurant, Dad handed me an article which he said I must read. It was from *New Idea* magazine and headed 'The Pregnant Boy of Kazakhstan'. The titular seven-year-old child had been born with his own twin inside him: 'The 2 kg foetus, 20 cm long, was attached to the blood vessels and had continued to grow... for seven years it lived like a parasite inside the boy's body, according to Dr Valentina Vostrikova, who led the team of surgeons.' Radioactive pollution was cited as a possible cause. The foetus died during the operation to remove it, and the boy said: 'I had a football inside me [making a round shape with his hands] but my mum has told me to stop talking about it.'

How, Dad asked me, did that boy end up with his twin growing inside him?

Why, I asked myself, did Dad cut out the article for me?

Maybe he remembered that I'd studied genetics. But whenever he gave me these clippings and notes, he always put his hand to his mouth in a gesture of keeping a secret and would rush to find a pocket in my clothing in which to bury the paper, as if we had a covert understanding, as if he were giving me cash without his wife knowing about it.

Later I sought a more serious source than the *New Idea*, and found a reference to the boy's condition: foetus-in-foetu. A BBC report suggested that the growth was a teratoma cyst, the remains of a misdeveloped twin. It was growing larger and causing the boy to be aware of it, but it wasn't a fully formed foetus, more like a cyst.

Dad's communications seemed ever more gnomic. Either he was trying to tell me something, or I was reading too much into every exchange.

Another news report caught my eye: a story about a 'tall strawberry blonde with blue eyes [who] struggled to work out why she looked so different from her family of short, dark-haired Mexicans'. The hospital had switched two children at birth in 1958; now these women, both of whom had felt out of step with the families they grew up in, were suing the hospital administration.

It was easy to find cases like this once you were attuned to spotting them. The story of Bobby Dunbar was featured on the popular NPR program *This American Life*. He went missing in 1912, during a camping trip in Louisiana with his parents. Eight months later a child found with an itinerant handyman was identified by the distraught parents as their missing Bobby, although another woman also claimed the boy was hers. The Dunbars went to court and won. The program followed the investigations of Dunbar's grand-daughter, who interviewed members of both families generations later, determined to find out if her grandfather really was Bobby Dunbar.

'If my past is wrong, Bobby Dunbar, all the legends, all the stories, and then all of a sudden you find out, well, that's not who your blood says you are,' she said, 'where does that leave me? If my grandpa isn't my grandpa, who am I?'

It was a question that disturbed others in her family, too. One relative said: 'She was really going up against the entire family...I felt like she is alienating everybody else... Why do this? Why do you need to do this? Nobody in the family wants to know.'

Then I saw the documentary *My Architect: A Son's Journey*, Nathaniel Kahn's 'search' for his father, Louis I. Kahn, who designed some of the most iconic twentieth-century American buildings. He died of a heart attack in the men's room of Penn Station in 1974, and the obituaries said he was survived by his wife Esther and daughter Sue Ann. But he had other children—one of whom was Nathaniel, whose mother, the landscape architect Harriet Pattison, had worked with his father.

In an interview the filmmaker said, 'I think you get to a point where your curiosity gets the better of you...There's always a risk of embarrassing yourself: here comes what appears to be a nearly middle-aged man asking questions that a child asks. That was difficult.' This echoed my feelings of pathos and embarrassment over the previous five years, knocking on the doors of strangers, asking if they might be related to me.

I found the film compelling but I couldn't help feeling envious that Nathaniel Kahn was searching for a man whose identity was known to him. His father had acknowledged him, had sent him postcards; he joined his mother at the funeral—although, as with another mistress who'd had a daughter to Louis I. Kahn, they were uninvited guests who believed nonetheless that they had a right to be there.

I wondered how the daughter and son of Kahn's mistresses had felt at encountering each other, and how they felt about the legitimate daughter sitting at the front with the official mourners. They must have searched each other's faces, observed the mothers, tried to see the common features inherited from their father.

I remembered a photograph of my sister and me standing in front of Mama's friend Isabel, like matryoshka dolls, my sister at the front. I was eight and she was four, and we were wearing outfits that Isabel had given us. I can still remember the sheen and softness of my blue-and-white paisley polished-cotton shirt and matching skirt. Someone looking at the photograph had said that we didn't look like sisters. Mama didn't dismiss the idea—*Oh darling*, she could have said, *sisters don't always look alike!*—but she did say that, whatever happened, we had to look after each other, for we were the only sisters we had.

//

A man is in hospital

A WEEK before my younger daughter's wedding, my sister and I heard from Dad's stepdaughter. Dad had again been admitted to hospital with heart failure.

We went to the hospital together. Believe me, two more ambivalent daughters you would never meet. Dad was propped up on pillows with an oxygen mask fixed to his face. When he saw us he pulled it off, shouting: 'These are my daughters, one is married but the other one isn't married anymore, but she's still young, who can look after her? I worry so much.'

This performance of The Good Father was directed at two comatose men in the beds opposite. It reminded me of one of Dad's previous roles: The Good Husband required him to rush to the kitchen sink when visitors came for Sunday afternoon tea and pretend to be washing up, a sight rarely seen at other times.

'Shh,' my sister said, replacing the mask. 'Relax—you're in hospital.'

'What do I need this for?' Dad said, pulling off the mask again.

'It's oxygen—it'll help you breathe,' she said. I saw her jaw clench.

'I'll tell you a joke!' he replied, pulling the mask away completely.

'A man is in hospital'—he was gasping now—'and he says, "Doctor, can you make me live to one hundred?" And the doctor says, "How old are you?" And the man says ninety-one, and the doctor says, "Do you smoke? Do you drink? Do you sleep with women?" And the man says no, and the doctor says, "Well, what do you want to live for?" Gettit? What does he want to live for if he doesn't sleep with women?'

'Dad, put the mask on.' I heard the insistence in my voice.

'Only one more joke,' he said, and now he was turning blue and coughing blood. 'A gynaecologist comes home and kisses his wife, and she says, "What are you kissing me for?" And he says'—Dad was shouting now, so the nurses came in—'"Because I haven't seen a face all day!" Gettit? Gettit?'

Now I was thinking of putting a pillow over his face. I pressed the oxygen mask on him instead, and he showed me his blood-stained tissue. I moved away, disgusted, and hoped my sister had more composure. (Re-reading this account, I realise I should've pocketed the tissue and sent it to a laboratory for genetic testing, but at the time I was not thinking strategically and instead I started to laugh, and my sister furrowed her brow.)

I was glad when Dad's wife arrived and told him how much she'd been missing him; I was astonished and pleased that someone loved him. I slunk off with my sister to drink coffee, and we agreed that we were not the right people to be giving directions about plans for his treatment or resuscitation. But he was telling jokes like a man who wanted to live—at least until the applause had subsided.

He'd been out of hospital for a few months after this episode when he called to tell me that his sixty-two-year-old heart specialist had just had a fatal heart attack. How had he outlived the doctor who'd told my sister he had grave doubts about Dad's capacity to pull through his last crisis?

Dad had been hard to find. He'd been going to restaurants and cafés all day, every day since he'd been released from his hospital bed. He'd come to my younger daughter's wedding straight from a big morning of telling jokes to people, and he could hardly stand up at the ceremony. He wasn't dressed for a wedding anyway, as he had decided not to come to the reception, which at first made me angry and then relieved.

He was the centre of his world. At my fiftieth-birthday party he arrived amid a blaze of old jokes, and I had reports of his stellar performances from those friends of mine he hadn't met before. His wife kept approaching the musicians, who were playing Django Reinhardt tunes, and asking them to stop, as she hated jazz.

Dad was now eighty-six. Would he ever die? We decided against the big lunch and instead gathered for afternoon tea at my sister's house. Dad came with his wife and her daughter and son-in-law. He sat at the end of the table and, as usual, took the presents we had given him and put them on the floor next to his chair, feigning a lack of interest. I insisted that he open them.

He told the same stories. My sister showed him a Moses action-man doll complete with detachable Ten Commandments that she'd bought in Hong Kong. Dad and his wife seemed engrossed at their end of the table, playing like children with the doll. Dad was especially enamoured of the commandments and Moses' staff, which was also detachable.

My oldest nephew and I talked about editing the commandments down to six, as the modern world was too fast for ten. I suggested removing the one about adultery. I couldn't remember if you were supposed not to covet your neighbour's ass or his wife or his wife's ass.

On New Year's Day my older daughter was passing through Melbourne on her way from Darwin, where she was now living, to New Zealand for a trekking holiday, so we called Dad to see if we could drop by for a cup of tea. She wanted to see him because she was worried that he might die soon. He told us he was having lunch and couldn't see us. We'd already eaten, we said, and would just have a cup of tea. He resisted, said he'd see her next time. Next time? He must have thought he would live forever, and I wondered if he might outlast me.

I'd heard that Max's wife was very sick. I thought that I'd be closer to being able to write my story if she were nearing death. I was like a vulture waiting for a body to fall. It was unedifying, I knew, but there it was.

I turned my mind to the war-crimes trial that Alan had mentioned his father—our father?—attending in Germany.

After which, Alan had recounted, Max came back saying, 'We got him.' Who the 'him' was, I had no idea, but I searched the internet for mentions of Max's name as a witness. I looked for Max Dunne and Majlech Adunaj in reports of the Frankfurt Auschwitz trials, which lasted from the end of 1963 to the middle of 1965, and found no clues.

Maybe it was a false trail? Maybe Max was trying to have a few weeks away from his wife and ended up on the Riviera for a holiday? It wouldn't be the first time a married man contrived a story to allow himself a spell away with a mistress. And it wasn't as if Max didn't have form.

One summer afternoon I sat on my veranda, looking across at my garden and the quiet street, and up at the blue, almost cloudless sky. I thought of how lucky I was to be here in this place and at this time, when it would have been so different had I been born somewhere else, twenty years earlier. I thought that this story might end prematurely, with the recognition that waiting for old people to die so that I might complete my investigations was unworthy.

I wondered how much anyone could know in this situation, and how important it really was to find a conclusion. It might be time to look to the future, instead of being obsessed with the past.

My son-in-law had survivor relatives who gave talks at the local Jewish Holocaust Museum and Research Centre. I'd asked them if there was a community response to the call to give evidence at the Frankfurt Auschwitz trial, and mentioned this in passing to my younger daughter.

She asked if I'd told them my story and I said no, that I'd just said I was researching for something I was writing. She asked if I was writing a book and I said of course I was, that she knew this. She told me she hadn't realised that I wanted to publish it. I shrugged her off, saying I'd wait till everyone was dead, and she replied, 'Including me?'

Dad was eighty-seven. Again we met at my sister's house for lunch. My older daughter was in Darwin; she and her husband were expecting their first child.

I'd bought a concrete duck for Dad at a garden-furniture place. I was running out of ideas. I'd looked for something suitable every year, yet his reaction to the last few presents had rattled me. He didn't read much anymore: he was in his own world. He had more or less constant lapses in under-standing; he was deaf, and just repeated his stories. Why a duck? I thought of the old Marx Brothers routine. Why not a duck? A concrete duck was as good as anything.

His wife was short with him now. She corrected him loudly and complained about him, but still she looked after him. Good on her, I thought. I couldn't do it.

That week, for my radio show I interviewed the poet and writer Jacob Rosenberg, whose memoir had just won the National Biography Award. He had worked with Mama in a Melbourne clothing factory before she went to work for the Dunne brothers. I'd seen him the week before, at a book launch, and we had talked about her. He said that she was like a nineteenth-century woman.

'Madame Bovary?' I asked.

Perhaps, he said. And he added that she was a bohemian at heart and had been trapped in a middle-class life.

I invited him to have coffee with me after our interview, and he sat with me at a little table in the busy open space of the atrium in the ABC headquarters. He remembered having lunch with Mama four or five times a week at the factory where they worked.

'She used to bring her lunch to my sewing machine and we talked. She was hungry for culture. And we would discuss books and I would recite for her my poems. And she would give me a kiss for a poem. She had thin lips but warm.'

They would sit close and talk—he described her as audacious and uninhibited, and I wondered how this manifested itself. I told him of my quest, as I knew I could trust him. He seemed a wise and thoughtful man, and I felt he would not disappoint me like the other elderly men I had been pursuing for my story. His friendship with her was platonic, he explained, and I asked why, thinking of the thin-lipped kisses, and he said it was perhaps because he was too immature at the time.

He asked why I wanted to know all this: wasn't it better to let sleeping dogs lie? I was interested in truth, I said, and he answered with a disquisition on truth. In response I quoted him something from his book: 'sometimes even the cruellest truth is preferable to the gentlest lie.'

He argued softly with me, back and forth. 'What does it profit us to know who made the world, was it God or was it the Big Bang?'

'In the scheme of things it's not important, but for me it's nice to know,' I replied. I ventured that it might be hard for him to understand, as he knew who his parents were. And anyway, I said, it was also about learning to trust your own intuition. I'd thought something was amiss for my whole life, and piecing together a story helped me begin to trust my own sense of reality.

Jacob's next book would be about his time as a prisoner in Auschwitz, when he became in his words 'a free animal', no longer having any family member to worry about, only himself. Thinking of this I became self-conscious: I was telling an Auschwitz survivor that he couldn't understand my little difficulty, in the face of everything he did understand.

He suggested I write all this down to relieve myself of it. Otherwise, he said, it would eat me up and make me unhappy. He told me to write a fictional account and not mention any names, and that it should be a detective novel.

I told him the interesting thing for me was that it was a search for the truth; it was about evidence and identity— why should it hide behind a cloak of fiction?

He became philosophical again about the meaning of truth. Before long his taxi arrived and he kissed me goodbye, heading off into the bright day.

A month later he sent me a card with a photo of a red rose on the cover. 'Darling Ramona,' he wrote, 'the enclosed picture is actually the cause of my belated thanks for your generosity and friendship. Love, Jacob.'

He had made a copy of a photo of Mama and him sitting together in a park, their faces framed by trees and lawn. They are both young, clear-eyed and smooth-skinned, with similar low-key smiles playing on their lips. Mama wears a light blouse with a Peter Pan collar under a darker tunic, and her hair is combed to one side. Jacob's tie needs straightening and he wears a knitted vest over a white shirt. Just a few years before, they had both faced certain death.

It is hard to read Mama's expression. Although she looks directly into the camera, the light seems to glance off the surface of her eyes; their depths are impossible to fathom.

12

What we had to tell

I WAS at an impasse. There was no one else I could call upon for more details of Max's life. I wrote to a handful of academics, trying to locate any testimony he'd given to war-crimes tribunals, and waited for a response. I could find nothing by perusing digital collections and suspected that what I wanted was probably filed under a misspelling in German in a dusty archive somewhere, in an ancient manila folder tied with red ribbon. I imagined these were the documents that would give me access to the voice of my father, or the voice of a man who was nothing to me.

Faced with silence, and a burning need to know more about Max, I decided I might be able to fill in some gaps using the testimonies of those who were likely to have been in the same place at the same time: people from Mława, who might have been with him in the Mława ghetto and transported with him to Auschwitz. I would shadow Max until I could find something more solid.

I went back to the memoir of the town written in Hebrew in 1949 by Dr Izhak Ze'ev Yunis and translated into English. When I had first found it I was only looking for a mention of Max's family name, but this time I read it properly. It is a charming account of Mława, which existed officially from 1429 on the long-range cattle-trade route between Russia and what eventually became Austria. From its early days the town had brewers, blacksmiths, potters, tailors, carpenters and butchers. Its fortunes declined in the seventeenth century and the Swedes invaded. Two fires ravaged the town in the eighteenth century, and it wasn't till the nineteenth and early twentieth centuries that things looked up. Mława was only seven kilometres from the border with Prussia: the establishment of a railway brought new prospects for business. Factories making leather goods, soap and oil, and then a big brewery, sprang up. With them came the smuggling of horses, gold watches, diamonds, silk and even people.

Jews were present in the town from the beginning, remaining part of its social fabric through good times and bad for over five hundred years. By the time Dr Yunis was growing up there were steam mills, a cement works, a cigarette-box manufacturer, an ink factory and a hub for wheat trading. Jews of all persuasions lived there: Ortho-dox, Zionist, secular, politically left and right; they formed a drama club and established a theatre, and there were newspapers catering for all shades of opinion.

Dr Yunis's account of the town reminded me of the scenes described by the great Sholem Aleichem and seen in *Fiddler on the Roof*: a time before the pogroms started.

In the centre of the market, on a large and wide base of stones, stood a pure white building built in the sixteenth century. The building was covered with red shingles. Hugging the four walls like a black belt was a Latin inscription: 'The same measure of justice applies to poor and rich, to citizens and new inhabitants, 1789.'

Above the roof a hexagonal grey turret with four round openings reached out to the skies, overlooking all four directions of the wind. The town clock was here.

Every quarter of an hour, its hoarse and familiar ring reverberated through the air. Children stood in the market place and looked at the clock's black hands slowly revolving around its white face and waited for the clock to strike.

Quite often the hands of the clock stood still. No peal was heard. Time seemed to have been arrested. A silent sadness filled the heart. The whole town impatiently waited for Moshe Wilner to get up, climb the tower and reset the clock. The town's time was in his hands.

I thought of the black-and-white silent films of the early twentieth century and imagined Charlie Chaplin as Moshe Wilner on a ladder, resetting the clock. Or maybe Harold Lloyd, hanging off the hands of the dial in the 1925 film *Safety Last*.

Dr Yunis spent his childhood exploring the nearby forests, watching the wooden water mills on the local rivers, smelling the flowers and enjoying the intrigues of bands of local children. Through his tale I learned of rabbis and tailors and ritual butchers and youth groups and markets and merchandise and crazy people. There were sages and politicians and theatre performances and characters who sounded like they were enacting old Jewish jokes—a man, his wife, the rabbi...Perhaps it was part memoir and part fiction, but reading it was strangely warming. It was a treat to imagine my connection to this working town, with its stories and documents and solid buildings.

Yunis said that by the 1930s people were leaving in droves for America and 'even Australia'. This was the period when Max's older brother Joseph left. Was Yunis thinking of him when he made that remark?

Of the almost five thousand Jews in Mława at the beginning of the war, only forty survived.

At the end of the Yunis text there are contributions from two other Mława residents that I hadn't noticed when I scanned the document the first time. Both were survivors of concentration camps and write about giving evidence to a war-crimes trial. There, in an account by Moshe Peleg (formerly Moshe Poltusker), a passage leaped out at me:

> Some of us who had been in the Mława ghetto were invited by the Germans to testify against the Nazi Policat. I will briefly describe this criminal. He was born on June 3, 1907, in Minserburg, East Prussia. He was commander of the gendarmes assigned to the Mława vicinity, who terrorized the Jews, among the rest, by ordering his dog to attack on command.
>
> People were invited from the United States, Australia, Germany and Israel to testify against him. From Israel were invited Hendel Avraham, Pesach Sheiman, Zelig Avraham, and myself, and also Ben Zion Bogen of Strzegow. Yosef Haussman

of Szrensk and Mordechai Purman of Rypin.

From the United States came Leibel Kozheni,
Harry (Hersh) Forma and Reuven Soldanar of
Szrensk; from Australia: Elimelech (Melech) Aduna.
We were all survivors of the extermination camps.

This is why you need to read things carefully and not rely
on name searches, I thought to myself, because Elimelech
(Melech) Aduna is Max Dunne. The misspelling of his original surname leaves off the 'j'.

I searched online for the trial details and found a record:

CASE NR. 755

CRIME CATEGORY: Other Mass Extermination Crimes

ACCUSED: Paulikat, Franz Ernst Walter *Life Sentence*

COURT: LG Arnsberg 710623

       BGH 711203

COUNTRY WHERE THE CRIME WAS COMMITTED: Poland

CRIME LOCATION: Striegenau

CRIME DATE: 42

VICTIMS: Jews

NATIONALITY: Polish

AGENCY: Police Gendarmerie Mielau

SUBJECT OF THE PROCEEDING: Shooting of a young Jewess
when she tried to switch from one row to another
within a group of Jews awaiting transport

PUBLISHED IN JUSTIZ UND NS-VERBRECHEN VOL. XXXV

I saw that Moshe Peleg had misspelled Paulikat as Policat, and
that the Police Gendarmerie was listed as being in Mielau
which was, between 1939 and 1945, the German name for the

Polish town of Mława. It was hard to know how I was ever going to get far with this story if the names and spellings changed depending on the teller of the tale and the writer of the document—but I felt extremely lucky to have a new direction to follow.

The case transfixed me. A young Jewess was shot 'when she tried to switch from one row to another within a group of Jews awaiting transport'. Was she trying to join her family or her sweetheart? Was she hiding contraband, or electing to stand with those she thought had a better chance of being put to work instead of to death? I wanted to find out as much as I could about this girl. She was trying to change her destiny—that much was clear.

And at last I had a lead in my search for Max's testimony. Not only might I find out more about what happened to him before he came to Australia: I might finally hear his voice in the pages of a transcript.

While I waited for a response to an email enquiry to the website where the trial details were listed, I read Moshe Peleg's description of embarking on his trip to Germany in May 1971 to testify. He tells of being nervous, as I suppose most of them were, about making the journey to Arnsberg in Westphalia, where the accused, Walter Paulikat, had taken up residence after the war. Paulikat had even served there in his old profession—he was the chief of police until he was recognised by a German man called Brecht, who reported Paulikat's whereabouts to those who dealt with war criminals in Germany.

All the former Mławan residents who were invited to testify in Arnsberg stayed together at the same hotel, so

Max must have been there with them. I wondered if he was nervous. Alan said he seemed afraid of men in uniforms, but this time the man in question was under arrest and the uniformed guards were on Max's side.

Moshe Peleg said he couldn't sleep or eat in anticipation of seeing the man he called 'the Nazi devil'. In the event, when he laid eyes on Paulikat the next day, Peleg collapsed and needed first-aid till he recovered, half an hour later. His testimony took two hours, and his fellow witnesses testified that same day and the next.

A month later, on 23 June 1971, Paulikat was sentenced to life imprisonment. Peleg writes that it made no difference to those who were killed, but those who travelled to Germany to testify could be satisfied that 'at least we helped bring the criminal to his punishment.'

That sounded like Alan's report of Max saying 'We got him' on his return from Germany. Now I felt as though I was finally getting somewhere with Max, even that I was closing in on him. I followed up my requests for information from the courthouse in Arnsberg, and waited to hear what discoveries my fresh luck would bring.

In the meantime, Dad was becoming demented, although no one used the term. In his late eighties, he was still going to the same coffee shop each morning, accompanied by his devoted but increasingly annoyed wife, to have the same thing for breakfast. Sometimes his cronies were there and they buzzed around his wife like elderly moths. They were still able to talk and joke with her, unlike poor Dad. He had become her child.

My older daughter and her husband had established

a routine of taking my granddaughter to see Dad in the coffee shop each week or two, and when they did they invited me along. I took the opportunity to build up my points, as if I were in a cosmic filial-rewards scheme. I wasn't sure what these points were going towards but I was happy to play with the baby, and I saw that Dad was captivated by her beauty and her sweetness. She was almost two and well practised in the art of coffee-house behaviour. She ate her frothy baby-chino with a spoon and held the glass in her little hands to finish off the milk.

At last Dad and I had something in common: delight in my granddaughter. 'Isn't he just gorgeous?' Dad said. Then, 'Look, she is drinking' and 'He likes to drink' and 'She has curly hair', and when he saw me he said, 'I think we have met before' and I told him, yes, I think we have met.

Mostly he spoke to me in Polish, a language he never taught me to speak. I tried to engage him in Yiddish, which I had taught myself with the aid of some lessons many years ago, but he no longer spoke back. And I realised that for the first time I was happy to meet him like this, with the baby on my knee and something else to think about besides our long and strange history together.

I liked him demented. It took the heat off me.

When I offered to help his wife, asking if I could do anything for them, and if she'd decided whether he needed more care than she was able to give, she told me, 'No, no—I am not ready to give up on him.' She said he followed her around the house and didn't want to go out much, other than their Saturday nights dancing at the German Club. Now she danced with other men and Dad stood on the sidelines. I admired her goodness and her loyalty to him. I was spared the burden of having to look after him in a way that he had never looked after me.

I went to the movies to see *The Counterfeiters*, a German–Austrian co-production: the story of the men who were part of Operation Bernhard, the attempt by the Nazis to supply counterfeit Allied currency and to induce the economic collapse of their enemies. One hundred and forty-four Jewish prisoners of many nationalities worked at the Sachsenhausen concentration camp near Berlin to produce such excellent counterfeit British pounds and American dollars that they were almost undetectable.

The film had great recreations of Weimar decadence and post-war recklessness, vividly depicting the mood of survivors. I could well imagine how I came to be born through desperation and rash judgement. The hard and distressed and partly demented group of survivors depicted in the film were like my parents' social circle.

Counterfeit. It looks just like the real thing but it's not authentic. That was me.

The men in *The Counterfeiters* had reminded me of Max and the hardness, the toughness, his son had described. Max was in Auschwitz for a long time because he had a 'good job in the infirmary'.

I returned to what I knew about him. Born on 23 December 1914, early in the other world war, he was almost thirteen years older than Mama. I was sure she would've been attracted to older men. Having lost her father when she was two months old, she'd been entranced by the sad but romantic story of him swimming across a cold river to be there for her arrival.

Long after she died I found out, in an unpublished memoir given to me by an Israeli-based second cousin of hers and translated from the Hebrew, that he died after receiving a blow to the head in a fight with neighbours from the village. He was a strong man who, according to this cousin, had been able to lift up a small horse, and when challenged to a fight he'd boasted that he could beat his opponent with one hand tied behind him. The fatal blow formed a blood clot in his brain, and he died a few days later. Mama and her brother were brought up by their mother and extended family—cared for and disciplined by all of them—and Mama loved both her grandfathers fiercely.

It didn't seem overly Freudian to think that she would look for a man who could father her and protect her, and with whom she might blossom. In Dad, she had a man who was damaged. He was the fourth and youngest child of a widow, doted on by his brother and sisters, and had great difficulty maturing into an adult. He was already twenty-one when the war started, and of course his experiences of it were traumatic and had changed his life's trajectory, but he was never going to be the man she craved.

Another year was heading towards its end and soon Dad would be ninety. Looking at my notes, I couldn't believe I'd been thinking about this story for ten years. I had little to do with Dad apart from the mornings in the coffee shop, and I ceded all responsibility for his health crises to my sister, who would work things out with his stepdaughter or wife.

I began to comb through the Visual History Archive of the Shoah Foundation, a collection of long and often traumatic interviews with survivors of the Nazi era. These people had given their testimonies to strangers behind the camera, sometimes telling them things they'd never told their own families. They had survived the war in extermination camps, or as hidden children, or by living in Aryan zones under false identities.

The French writer Robert Antelme (the husband whose return from the camps Marguerite Duras writes of in her book *The War*) discusses in his remarkable memoir *The Human Race* the disconnect between knowledge and the capacity to speak of it:

> [D]uring the first days after our return [from the camps], I think we were all prey to a genuine delirium. We wanted at last to speak, to be heard. We were told that by itself, our physical appearance was eloquent enough; but we had only just returned, and with us we brought back our memory of our experience, an experience that was very much alive, and we felt a frantic desire to describe it such as it had been. As of those first days, however, we saw that it was impossible to bridge the gap we discovered opening up between the words at our disposal and our experience which, in the case of most of us, was still going forward within our bodies...no sooner would we begin to tell our story than we would be choking over it. And then, even to us, what we had to tell would start to seem unimaginable.

There were thousands of interviews to watch in the Shoah Foundation's archive, filed according to languages and war experiences and places of imprisonment, and it was overwhelming. For most of my life I'd avoided war stories or documentaries showing horrific scenes, and I'd learned never to ask Mama or Dad or their friends to tell me what had happened to them, for fear of stirring up memories and tears and anger. But this video resource gave me a chance to sit and hear, and to move between people and countries, and when I'd had too much I could press pause and go away without hurting the feelings of the teller.

I started by searching for names of family members. That there was somewhere, somehow, a survivor of my mother's large family who she'd not been in contact with was a romantic fantasy, but I found a man with the same last name as her: Leon Kawer, pronounced *Ka-ver*, from the word for 'coffee seller' in Polish or Yiddish. He was from Poland and, along with his family, had ended up in Paris before the war. His testimony was sometimes dull—but when he spoke about how he made false documents for others to use, I was riveted.

He told of finding sympathetic priests, who would in turn point out sympathetic mayors, who would stamp the correct things on documents that showed other, real people's identities alongside the photographs of Jews who were to assume and live under these identities. I had a rush of wanting him to be my father, because he was clever and brave. I looked up at his image on the screen and I felt six years old, vulnerable but protected. He might have been related to me, but equally his name might just mean that someone in his family imported coffee. How fickle of me to be so easily seduced into wanting this new, absent father! The feelings passed in moments.

I started looking in the archive for people who had been born in and around Mława, and who may have been with Max in the ghetto there, or made the journey with him to Auschwitz and beyond. I already had the names of some of his fellow witnesses in the trial of Walter Paulikat, and I found that two of them had been interviewed by the Visual History Archive. While I waited for their videos to be released to me, I sought out interviews with others who may have had the same kind of experiences as Max. I found Henry Coleman, born Henoch Kalma.

He was in the Mława ghetto in 1943 and was transported to Auschwitz, where he was tattooed with the number 76344. Max's number was 76200, so I suspected that they were there at the same time. I knew they would have been tattooed in alphabetical order, A before K. I imagined Max being tattooed while Henry was waiting for the 143 people between them to file through. How strange to be thinking about the tattoo on the arm of a man who had nothing to do with me because the number was close to the one on the arm of a man who also might also have nothing to do with me. I was painting by numbers. How pathological was this drive to connect—with a father figure, any father figure.

Henry Coleman said that when the Russians liberated them he shot a German SS man wearing civilian clothing whom he recognised, and soon after that he rode a bike because he loved bicycles. A shooting and a bike ride. I watched the rest of his testimony and waited for a mention of people he might have met.

After the war Henry went to America and made a new life there. 'And this is my story,' he said, towards the end of the video, and he cried, as he had now and then during the telling. I thought of the way Dad would cry when he remembered the war years and the things he had seen, but Henry was clearer and less self-absorbed. He told of his grandchildren asking him about the numbers on his arm and how they came to be there.

'There were some bad men,' he began, his head to one side, as if rehearsing how he might answer, 'and they killed people. But how can you explain'—and now he looked through his tears directly at the camera—'explain to a little child what happened? What happened to all the little Jewish children?'

I spent days with the different testimonies, compelled and horrified. As I watched, I censored the stories that I couldn't listen to—I always encountered ones I wished I hadn't heard—while looking for clues from survivors from Mława, in case they named the object of my interest. When the testimony became too hard to take, I left my desk to play with my grandchildren for an hour or so.

On one occasion I watched a man talking about an incident he witnessed in the Mława ghetto, when a German soldier offered a piece of chocolate to a starving baby in its mother's arms. The survivor thought he was witnessing a rare example of kindness; he thought the soldier was an angel. I had to stop the video there. I was finding it hard to breathe. From the way the man was talking I knew that something awful was coming.

I fled. I sat with my youngest grandchildren, the twins,

and the little girl tried to feed me her corn kernels and her brother took bites out of my tomato. As I watched them, I thought of what happened to all the little Jewish children, and I couldn't bear it. I wondered if not knowing something is better than knowing too much. I dreaded hearing the stories but I owed it to the tellers to listen.

I went back to the man's testimony. Rabbi Lipman Radzic was his name. As I expected, the rest of the story was about the murder of the child by the German soldier who offered the chocolate. The soldier put a pair of gloves on, in order to hold the child by the feet and smash its head against a water pump. And, having killed the child, the man shot the mother in the face as she pulled out her hair in grief.

There it was. I had heard this kind of story before, I told myself, and I was used to it. I breathed again, understanding that I was not going to be newly horrified.

Jacob Rosenberg's testimony was in the archive, too. He was, as you would expect of a writer, a natural storyteller. I searched the end of the recording, where he spoke of his life after the war, in case he talked about being in Melbourne and knowing Mama.

Perhaps, I thought, it was self-absorbed to be looking for places where his story merged with mine. But isn't that the way it is for all of us? We are the summation of all the stories, some known and most unknown, and all the lives that come before us.

Much later, I watched the video once again, this time from the beginning. Jacob describes his poor but happy family before the war: 'I cannot remember a time when we were not singing...We were readers...Whenever father bought a book it was like a celebration, like an extra member came into the family.'

He was calm, analytical, reasoned. In his accounts of his time as a slave labourer in the Łódz ghetto and in Auschwitz, he told of his method of keeping warm by thinking about fire, and noted that his poetry was full of imagery of snow and frost, as those times left an indelible mark. He told the story of a man who, forced to hang his own son, elected to hang himself as well: one noose for two heads.

The essential thing for survival, he said, was to hope, and not to think. Thinking was devastating. And that making sense out of such a senseless atrocity was a great art. For me, he said, the written word, my poetry, is my museum. I walk in there, and it's alive. Survivors, he said, understood that there is a language beyond words.

Could I really hope to understand Max, a man I had never known, a survivor, without grasping the language beyond words?

13

A goatskin jacket
and a bearskin hat

WHEN, in the 1960s, we moved from our one-bedroom flat in St Kilda to a three-bedroom triple-fronted solid-brick place in North Balwyn—from a seedy urban beachside suburb to one with leafy middle-class respectability—Dad was deputised to take me to Jewish Sunday school. Temple Beth Israel in Camberwell was a reform congregation with services held mostly in English. The Hebrew prayers and songs sounded almost Presbyterian. There were no great beards or side locks or black garb, and men and women sat side by side instead of the women being relegated to the area upstairs or behind a curtain, as they are in Orthodox congregations.

I was excited to be getting out of the house on Sunday mornings, yet shy. I knew nobody.

On the first Sunday I could hear Dad getting worked up over something as he spoke with the school officials. His voice was getting louder and higher even than his usual bellowing tones.

'Of course she is Jewish!' he was saying.

'But is her mother Jewish?' they asked.

'Of course her mother is Jewish!'

'But is she adopted?'

'How can you say she is adopted?'

But I was so blond: how could I be of the faith? These not-so-religious Jews had taken all the Aryan propaganda to heart. I was fair and blond, so I must be part gentile. The fuss made me feel inauthentic, a state in which I would find myself again many times over the years.

Thinking about the conversation now, I wonder if they were just expressing their suspicions as they looked at Dad: at his black hair and brown eyes and swarthy complexion. Maybe they smelt a rat?

I learned then that people look like their mothers and fathers, sometimes more like one than the other. Their hair, their eyes, their skin, even the shape of their legs. I had never thought about it. But I began to notice the differences in our family.

When I asked Mama, she said that my sister took after Dad—who shaved each day but had a reddish beard. This seemed an intimate fact for Mama to know about Dad, and I remember feeling embarrassed by it. She went on to explain how, when she was a little girl, she had hair just like mine.

There was no way she could prove it. I had to take her word for it and not press the point. Mama seemed to know many things—those she told and those she didn't. She was much smarter than Dad, who just worked in the factory, told jokes and played cards. She read books, sometimes in

French or in Polish. And, even though she took in piecework from clothing factories and I heard the treadle machine's whirring as the pedal rocked under her feet late into the night, she always gave the impression of being wise. That's what the matter with her was, Dad would say. She read too many books.

When I was a teenager Mama let me read the books she had devoured: the banned ones (*Lady Chatterley's Lover, Ulysses, The Group, Portnoy's Complaint*), and those by the feminists and the sociologists (Simone de Beauvoir, Betty Friedan, Alvin Toffler). Did she give me *The Double Helix* by James D. Watson, a hugely popular book in 1968? I don't think so. It was technical and I was keen on chemistry, so it was probably my choice. There was a memorable subplot about the female X-ray crystallographer Rosalind Franklin and how men played down her vital role in determining the structure of DNA.

I read of the mysterious, beautiful dance of the deoxyribonucleic acids, the DNA double helices, and learned about how they unzipped and transferred all their information to the new generation of cells. This was the way all kinds of things appeared and reappeared from one generation to the next. It was the unbroken chain that connected me with my antecedents and with theirs before them, all the way back as far as I could think. This elegant molecular chain of events led to your hair and your eyes and the shape of every body part, and I fell in love with its mystery and the stories it evoked.

I studied science at high school, then at university. In first year we studied the way the blood groups were inherited. I was B positive, my mother was O positive, and so was my sister, and that meant that my father had to be B positive, too. But he wasn't. I raised it with my laboratory supervisor and got a story about the rate of false positives. It was, thinking back, a remarkably insensitive experiment to do with a group of students. Maybe it isn't done quite so freely now we know that about ten per cent of children are not the issue of their official fathers.

I'd already told my supervisor about the simian crease on my right hand, which can be indicative of Trisomy 21 or Down syndrome. But he looked at me and rolled his eyes, as I clearly didn't have any other Trisomy 21 features and had no intellectual deficit.

Now I see that, however unconsciously, I was on the cusp of embarking on this investigation, but at the time the blood testing didn't trigger any urgent interest in me to follow up the mystery. My mother seemed uninterested in my laboratory experiments, perhaps trying to put me off the scent. I wonder now if she was troubled by her daughter's pursuit of studies in heredity and the way genes are shared in families. By then, though, Mama was gravely ill and my father's blood group was the least of my concerns and most likely of hers, too.

Years after she died, I returned to my musings. Where did the fairness and blue eyes come from? Why were the Sunday school officials so suspicious? How did I get to look like this if I was a descendant of a group of desert-wandering Middle Eastern Semites—why didn't I have black hair and deep-brown eyes?

I read Arthur Koestler's *The Thirteenth Tribe*. Here was

the story of the Khazar Empire, which ruled the Western Steppe—the region that stretches from the mouth of the Danube River along the north shore of the Black Sea, across the lower Volga and eastwards to the Altai Mountains—between the seventh and tenth centuries CE. It was a confederation of Turkic, Iranian and Mongol tribes who lived in what is now southern Russia, north of Georgia and east of Ukraine, a major connection between the Middle East, Russia and China, ruling the western end of the Silk Road.

The Khazars were a buffer between the Christian Byzantine Empire and the Muslim Umayyad Caliphate, and to fulfil this role the royal and aristocratic families of Khazaria, rather surprisingly, converted to Judaism. Surprising to me, because Judaism is not a proselytising religion and I'd never heard of a mass conversion like this. But there had been Jews in the Caucasus in the centuries before Jesus of Nazareth, and they were there after the increase of trade along the Silk Road and the decline of Judea in the first to seventh centuries CE.

Greco-Roman Jews and Mesopotamian Jews also found their way to Khazaria, and the conversion of the Khazars to Judaism in the eighth century increased their flow to the region. Just how many Khazars beyond the ruling class converted is unclear, but in any case the empire lasted for four hundred years, till the Mongols came.

What a story! It had all the elements of the Arabian Nights: mysterious travellers from abroad, kings and aristocrats, conversions to a foreign faith, topped off with a Mongol invasion.

Koestler theorised that the fair- or reddish-haired, blue-eyed Ashkenazi Jews of Eastern Europe were directly descended from these wild men and women of the Caucasus, who fled eastwards following the collapse of their empire. In the fourteenth century they met the exiled Jews from the Spanish Inquisition as they were making their own way north and east through Italy, France and Germany. By the middle of the sixteenth century, most of the world's Jews lived in Poland.

The Khazar theory of the founding Ashkenazi population was challenged by the Rhineland theory, which had Jews from Rome (following the destruction of the Second Temple in Jerusalem, in 70 CE, by Roman troops under Titus) merging eastwards through the Rhine Valley and into Eastern Europe. Here they may have met the Jewish remnants of Khazaria, although there are debates about the reliability of the original sources for the Khazar story.

Whichever way the populations arrived at their meeting point, the darkness of the Sephardic Jews mixed with the fairness of the Ashkenazi Jews. And if we fast-forward to the years after the Holocaust, there was a higher percentage of fairer survivors than darker ones. Fairer Jews could more easily hide in the Polish population, with its predominantly Northern European looks. It made sense to me. After all, this was the story of Mama's survival. She was able to hide in Warsaw during the Nazi occupation using forged Aryan documents because she could pass as a Polish Catholic.

What's more, it was redolent of a classic experiment in population genetics that I'd studied at university. The light-coloured peppered moths of Britain had an advantage over their dark-coloured brethren, because they could merge into the bark of birch trees common in their habitat, making it hard for predatory birds to see them and to pick them off. They bred happily.

During the industrial revolution, the air became polluted with soot and the surfaces of the trees were blackened. Now it was the turn of the dark moths to survive in favour of the light moths, which stood out against the sooty tree trunks. After 1970, when air-pollution regulations limited the output of soot from factories, the trees lightened, and the light moths regained pre-eminence.

I'd always been fascinated by this, and now I understood why. It was intrinsically interesting, but I also saw that I was like the light-coloured moths, a product of the vicissitudes of the environment of my antecedents, of the luck of the draw.

The Khazar story drew me in, offering answers to questions that had been nagging at me for decades. I wanted to discover what the Khazars looked like. I soon found, in several sources, references to them being handsome, with reddish hair, white skin and blue eyes.

I pored over maps of the kingdom and imagined an ancestor in boots and a long kaftan, with her hair plaited—and riding a wild horse, naturally. I used Google Earth's satellite photos to swoop down on the lands of the Khazars from the safety of my home, testing to see if one landscape or another held a particular race memory for me. One mountain village looked much like the next, and much like the small Polish hamlets I'd seen in my travels. The larger towns were mixtures of traditional churches and Soviet-style public buildings. Nothing looked like a yurt, and the closest I ever got to seeing one was the writers' retreat in the gardens at Charlotte Square at the Edinburgh Book Festival.

By this stage I'd long accepted that my experiments with Alan's DNA had not been conclusive: I would not be able scientifically to confirm my relationship to Max. But ten years had passed since I sent off my DNA sample, and it was now possible to send another sample of cheek scrapings to a laboratory in the USA running the Genographic Project. Samples from people from all over the world were being collected and analysed for both Y chromosomal geographic movements (the Y chromosome is handed intact from father to son through all generations) and those carried on mitochondria, the energy factories of our cells, handed down from mothers to both men and women.

While I was unsure about who my father was, I was certain about my mother. And I was entranced by the idea that whatever genes were inside the mitochondria of my Ur-mother were in every cell of mine, too. Even more exciting was the discovery that geneticists could now trace the mitochondrial genes to particular geographic regions and communities, and offer a paleoanthropological theory about the journeys that had been undertaken by human populations with those particular markers, all the way back to the groups of *Homo sapiens* who ventured out of Africa between sixty thousand and 125,000 years ago.

Granted, it was at quite a remove from my here-and-now, but it was consoling to imagine the certainty of the connection. My mitochondrial DNA was given to me by

my mother and to her by hers, as far back as I could visualise. And if the genes could tell me a story of travel and
settlement, it would be more than the search for my father
had revealed.

Some months later, when the results of the test came
back, I learned that my mitochondrial DNA was derived
from, led directly to, a woman whom scientists had named
Katrine (or K), one of seven 'mitochondrial Eves' described
by Bryan Sykes in his book *The Seven Daughters of Eve*.

Sykes imagined that K, the woman I was connected
to by an unbroken chain of female relatives, would have
been on a great plain now covered by the North Adriatic
Sea, around fifteen to twenty-five thousand years ago. It
wasn't hard to imagine her descendants following bands
of game animals eastwards for twenty thousand years and
ending up as Khazars at the end of the first millennium CE.
I looked at the map, and traced her journeys and those of
her descendants.

I scoured the literature for anything I could find about
this K group, and to my surprise I discovered I had another,
more recent relative to meet. And a male relative, at that. On
the direct line of mitochondrial genetics from K to me was
Ötzi the Iceman.

Ötzi was the body, now rather withered and desiccated,
that two German climbers found frozen and half-covered
in ice in September 1991 as they descended the Fineilspitze
in the Ötztal Alps, near the Italian–Austrian border. He
was well preserved but clearly had been there for a while,
judging by his clothing and equipment. Subsequently he
was dated as being between five thousand and 5,350 years

old. Because his body had been deep-frozen so long, it was possible not only for his DNA to be recovered but also for paleo-forensic experts to work out all kinds of things about him, by analysing what he was carrying when he died and the state of his body.

I found pages devoted to Ötzi on the website of the museum in Bolzano, northern Italy, where he is now housed. As I stared at his creepy form I found myself looking for traces of myself in his hair and what was left of the shape of his face. How bizarre to be combing this corpse for evidence of connection—but he was a long-lost relative, and I was obsessed with finding myself a branch, any branch, of a family tree to perch upon.

I was not alone here. A large percentage of people with the K connection are Ashkenazi Jews: 1.7 million Jews alive today share the same genetic fingerprint. Brushing the 1,699,999 others aside, I read what I could about my old cousin Ötzi. Years of experts examining his body have given us a marvellous reconstruction of his story and especially the last day or so of his life.

For a Neolithic man forty-six years was elderly, and Ötzi was shortish at 152 centimetres tall. He had broken a couple of ribs in the past; he had arthritis, some fleas and intestinal whipworm; and he had cuts on his hands and torso. But what he would have been most bothered by on his last day was the arrowhead deep in his shoulder which, in addition to a head injury, caused his death.

Analysis of isotopes and enamel in Ötzi's teeth and bones told of his growing up in the Eisack Valley and spending his adult life further west. The day before he died, he swallowed some pollen from around the Schnals Valley, and then had another meal which contained pollen from a lower region. His last meal, eaten three hours before he died, was high up again, near a sub-alpine forest.

He was wearing three layers of skins and grasses, a belt holding up his loincloth and leggings, a goatskin jacket, and a bearskin hat. The stitching on these items of clothing was carefully tailored; his shoes were made of skins of calf, deer and bear, and lined with grass. He had with him a large copper axe with a handle of yew wood; a longbow staff and arrows; a dagger and a sheath; a bark container for charcoal; and a belt with flints, tinder, and a tool for working on the arrows and unfinished longbow. He was also carrying a string net, perhaps for trapping birds.

Like Max, he was tattooed. He had fifty-two markings at various points on his body, including a cross on the inside of his left knee, and numerous parallel lines above his kidneys and across his ankles. They were not produced with needles but by rubbing charcoal into fine skin incisions. There was speculation about these being found at points of wear and tear on his body, and possibly where medications may have been applied or at acupuncture points. But there they were, more mysterious and less shocking than Max's marking, and on a man to whom I could claim to trace a definite line of descent.

Ötzi might have been a herdsman driving sheep and goats around his valley, well prepared for hunting and gathering some of his food, repairing his tools (his damaged arrow shaft) and clothing, and spending days away, making campfires at night. But in his last few days he'd been on the run, descending from up high, possibly to his settlement, then leaving again to scale the mountain to a much higher level. Wounds on his hands and head tell of a fight just before his death. His pursuers must have caught up with him, the arrow was shot—and now I could see it behind an unhealed wound, in an X-ray sitting on my computer screen.

Analysis of Ötzi's clothing, broken arrowheads and knife revealed the blood of four people: two different individuals on his arrow, a third on his knife blade and, on the left side of his jacket, the fourth. One theory is that he shot two people with his arrowhead and carried the wounded body of another on his shoulder. A rival theory suggests that he was the object of a ritual sacrifice: otherwise, why had he been left with such a valuable axe? Here he was on my screen, an accident of time and weather and nature and luck, having preserved his last few days in the vessel of his body; and here I was, nearly five and a half thousand years after his death, trying to piece together his story and relate it to my own.

A few years later the Genographic Project was offering an even more detailed analysis. I sent them another sample. After waiting a few months I got the result. I could claim an identification as a member of the subclade K1a1b1a. I shared this subclade with a fifth of other Ashkenazim, seldom with other populations, although it was present in some Romani groups. Was I now a gypsy, too? Ötzi and I shared the mitochondrial marker 10978G, in common with everyone in the K1a1b1a subclade.

I read in the report's accompanying notes that 'most members of this group stem from a group of individuals who moved northward out of the Near East. These women crossed the rugged Caucasus Mountains in southern Russia, and moved on to the steppes of the Black Sea.' How did they do it? Who did they travel with, and what did they take with them? The trips would have taken many generations, after establishing a camp and settling into an area, hunting it out and moving on. I could be as sure of my connection with them as I was with Mama, the mitochondrial DNA link unbroken.

Following this line of thought, I began to think that it might not matter who my father was. I could imagine myself fifty thousand years back, connected to women who lived around the Mediterranean and whose offspring found their way up to the Volga region, through what became Persia and southern Russia. Or perhaps they were already settled there and met a Jewish trader from the south, coming up through Turkey with an eye on the Silk Road, the geography of multiple genetic mixing over centuries. I have no idea when any of them might have set off.

The Ur-mothers were deep in the past, yet it seemed to be a solid connection to think about. Pinning down exactly what a feeling of connection meant was tricky. When I met Australians overseas, I felt connected by shared language and some shared aspects of culture. Provided they were not too different from me, I could feel they understood me a little, at least. But what about a Romanian woman who had the same subclade connection to the foremothers through mitochondrial DNA: was there more to connect me with her than with a random Englishwoman who shared my language and perhaps my cultural references? This business of identity was fraught with both confusions and delicious possibilities.

The results in the report reflected not just the mitochondrial DNA from my Kıaıbıa line, but the rest of the DNA in my cell nucleus, too. I learned that my genes derived from populations around the Mediterranean (fifty-seven per cent), Southwest Asia (twenty-three), Northern European (seventeen) and Sub-Saharan Africa (two).

The largest component was the signal from the Neolithic populations expanding outwards from the Middle East about eight thousand years ago from the western part of the Fertile Crescent. The next component was picked up when ancestors moved from the eastern part of the Fertile Crescent, as Europeans mixed with those from Southwest Asia. The smallish seventeen per cent Northern European fraction is most likely from the earliest hunter-gatherers of Europe, who were making a late transition to agriculture. The two per cent Sub-Saharan African fraction was found mostly in Bantu speakers, but small numbers are found in Tunisian and Egyptian populations. Perhaps the strangest results of all were the distribution of my hominid genes: 1.8 per cent Neanderthal, 3.8 Denisovan, the rest *Homo sapiens*.

I learned that my gene distribution was most like a reference population of current-day Bulgarians, followed by a population of current-day Lebanese. This, I felt, accorded with what I'd discovered so far—my lineage derived from a group of Middle Eastern Jews who travelled across Turkey and into the Caucasus and the south of Russia, mixing a bit with the indigenous women there, thus picking up my Kıaıbıa mitochondrial DNA from my mitochondrial mothers, and forming the cultural and religious foundations of the Ashkenazi population that I trace my more recent family history from.

I thought about how tanned I could get in summers past, a nod to my mostly Mediterranean skin. And about my two per cent Sub-Saharan African genes, and whether my curls were from there. Since Max and Alan and their families were all from the same small region of Eastern Europe as the rest of my family, we were all as related to each other as any second or third cousins could be.

I was relieved to have so few Neanderthal genes, as some people have up to three per cent, although I was worried that this was a speciesist attitude of which I should not be proud. I didn't find the reconstructions of their appearance from skeletal remains particularly attractive, but evidence from Neanderthal burials suggests that they may have been sympathetic beings who cared for their injured confreres, and buried their dead with ritual and flowers. They seemed simple, and sweet. I reproached myself. Dad's voice came back to me: *You can pick your friends but you can't pick your relatives!*

And wasn't I trying to do just that, engaged in a giant act of brushing aside those relatives with whom I could not make a connection and searching for people who might stand in their place? As fascinating as I found the story of Ötzi and the last days of his life, I knew that the five thousand years since his death had sanitised the story for me and made it hard to feel genuinely connected to him, despite our common genes which I carried in every one of my cells.

My desire to fill out Max's story took me back to a time which was much better documented, but which also contained the horror and fetid smell of recent events. I was drawn, despite my misgivings, to immerse myself in it once again.

14

A good job in the infirmary

I NEEDED a thread to follow through the labyrinth of Max's Auschwitz story. All I knew of my quarry was the tattooed number on Max's arm: 76200. I'd been searching the archives for testimonies of men who were in the same 'transport' from the ghetto in Mława to Auschwitz. I'd found Leon Kruger, whose number was 76370; Rubin Soldaner, 76619; and several others, all numbered in alphabetical order. Order was everything: *Alles in Ordnung.*

Kruger made a point that struck me. He said that after he'd spent some time in the camp, his number showed that he was 'an old-timer'. It was a miracle to live in Auschwitz for a day, much less a month or a year. Even German soldiers viewed such an old number with something like respect. The man who had this number inked on his arm must be tough, strong and lucky. So Max was tough, strong and lucky, too.

Rubin Soldaner was one of Max's fellow witnesses in the Paulikat trial, but I might have missed his testimony had I been looking for his name in the Yunis memoir of Mława, where he was referred to as Reuven Soldanar. I was

constantly being led off track by careless or phonetic spellings, and changes of names and identities. Soldaner emerged
as I searched for mentions of tattoo numbers I had arbitrar-
ily chosen to be between 76000 and 77000. I was unnerved
to be using the Nazi classificatory system for my research,
but what else could I do?

As it turned out, Rubin Soldaner's story was important,
the stuff of the best courtroom dramas. Born in the village
of Szrensk, twenty-five kilometres from Mława, he was
five years younger than Max. He was chosen to work as a
personal slave for Walter Paulikat, who was in charge of the
ghetto. Soldaner cleaned Paulikat's quarters and his office,
chopped wood for him, shined his boots, prepared his
shaving water in the mornings, groomed and fed his four
horses, and mucked out the stables. He later reported being
beaten constantly by Paulikat, no matter how diligently
he'd done his tasks.

Once, he had asked why these beatings continued and
Paulikat answered by showing him one of his hands with
half a finger missing. He'd fought in the Spanish Civil War
on Franco's side, he said, and his finger had been bitten off
by a man he called 'a Jewish Communist', so Soldaner had to
pay for it.

At the trial, when Soldaner was giving evidence, Paulikat
said that he didn't recognise the man who claimed to be his
personal slave.

Soldaner reported saying, 'You don't remember me?
You used to beat me up every single night because a Jewish
guy bit off half your finger. Let him raise his hand and show
the court—see if half a finger is missing.'

Paulikat was asked to raise his hand, and everyone in the court could see that Soldaner was correct.

They gave Paulikat a life sentence. 'You know what a life sentence is?' Rubin Soldaner says in his testimony. 'He had to register his presence in the police precinct each week, and that was his life sentence.'

I wondered if Max ever learned of this, or if he continued to believe that the group of survivors who'd joined together to testify in the trial had 'got him'. Paulikat would merely have visited his former workplace once a week, making a mockery of the idea of ongoing punishment. Perhaps he continued to have a beer with his old colleagues, silently cursing the inconvenience of having to report to them while making a joke of his sentence.

Rubin Soldaner said he'd been in Auschwitz between November 1942 and January 1945, after which he was rounded up and taken on one of the infamous 'death marches'. When the Russians were rumoured to be coming to liberate the camp, those in charge sought to cover up what went on there. Six thousand prisoners were marched the twenty-five kilometres to Dachau; half of them were killed along the way.

I didn't know if Max was on the march. Some stayed behind in the camp, too sick to walk, even though the Nazis told them they'd buried gelignite around the camp perimeter, so that all the evidence of the atrocities would be obliterated.

More delicate people, Rubin Soldaner said, couldn't handle life in Auschwitz. He said that if your life in Poland was rough before the war, you had a better chance of survival in the camp. He was living in Block 7A with many others from Mława. They were taught to be bricklayers and plasterers, in order to build extensions to the camp. He was proud, in a way, that those buildings were still standing decades after the war.

If you knew someone who worked in 'Canada', the warehouse that processed clothes and belongings—the goods and valuables of those who arrived in Auschwitz and were stripped of everything, including their hair, and then sent to be murdered—they might steal something and trade it. You might have a chance of getting extra food, which meant extra time, and perhaps you might live till the war was over. This black economy was punishable by death, but those who knew how to trade and who were lucky were able to sustain themselves.

'Everything was a miracle,' Rubin Soldaner said.

Alan had told me that Max made uniforms in Auschwitz, but I needed to check if this was possible. Maybe he worked as a bricklayer with the other men from Mława who survived with him to testify at Paulikat's trial? I also needed to investigate Alan's report that Max had 'a good job' in the infirmary. How did he get it? What might a tailor have done in an infirmary?

Perhaps I was being too literal. Some survivors said in their testimonies that they'd lied about having certain skills and had watched what others did, learning on the job. They'd survived not because they were trained, but because they were skilled bluffers and fast learners.

If you had food, you survived; if you didn't, you died. If you got sick, you died. One of the men whose testimony I heard wore a stolen suit from 'Canada' under his striped camp uniform. On the forced march to the camp at Dachau they stayed in a barn for the night. He left before dawn under cover of darkness and shed his striped pyjamas. 'I kept walking,' he said. 'I was now a civilian.'

Hersh Forma—or Harry Forman, as he later became— was another of Max's group to give evidence against Pauli-kat. He was also in Block 7A in Auschwitz, and helped build the women's camp and the SS camp. He said that everything in Auschwitz was done by prisoners: the baking, the slaughtering of meat. 'A camp is a city, it's a big place.' He talked of his number, too: 'Our numbers made people realise we were "old soldiers" and people knew we were experienced.'

Harry Forman said that the decision to go on the death march was the worst one of his life, as he almost died in the four months between leaving Auschwitz and finally being liberated by the Americans. He said that the Gestapo did not give up trying to kill them till the last possible minute.

I didn't know what he meant by the worst decision of his life: did he have agency in deciding whether to stay or go? Those left in the camp were the sick and the dying, and typhus was common, but in the end they were liberated nine days after the march began—much earlier than those who were marched away from the advancing Russians. Maybe Forman was ill and could have stayed, but thought his chances were better with the marchers?

After the war the survivors roamed the countryside looking for food, first asking for it and then, when they were denied, killing chickens they'd taken from local farmers. Now the Allied forces were the occupiers, and no one dared complain. The remnant people of the camps registered for rations and got coupons from various places. They used the survival skills they had learned in Auschwitz.

I thought about Max and how he had lived in the years before his arrival in Melbourne to set up with his brother. He must have thought, as Mama did, that Australians had no idea how hard life had been for the new arrivals, and could not imagine what they had seen and survived. On reaching Melbourne, Mama thought she had fallen into a child's garden of verses. How could his brother or any of those who had escaped early begin to understand Max's story? Like me, they wouldn't have grasped the language of silence that Jacob Rosenberg had described.

Fitfully, I began searching Google with the keywords 'Auschwitz + infirmary + tailor'. The photographs I found made me queasy and my gut exploded in liquid reaction. I remembered Dad showing me photographs like this once when I was a child. He was trying to get me to sympathise with him, to understand him, but I was only eight.

I still think he was wrong in doing this. Mama was furious with him. After that day, I was afraid of the wardrobe in which he kept the glossy commemorative magazine with the gold-embossed Hebrew letters on the cover. I wanted the wardrobe doors to be closed, any wardrobe door in any room, especially at night when I was going to sleep.

Curiosity about my beginnings now took me to the depths of the filth and depravity of the infirmary at Auschwitz. Was this where Mengele carried out his experiments with twins and typhus? Where babies were killed at birth, and others died from phenol injected directly to the heart? Maybe these were the scenes that Isabel remembered when she told me about being punished for not wanting to have children and for having abortions. I found it hard to sleep and, when I did, I sometimes had nightmares.

I dreamed I was in my white cotton nightie, riding a bicycle to meet a friend. I passed by a paddock with a large horse. I knew it had something to do with me, but at the same time it was not my responsibility. I saw that there were scars and welts on the horse's flanks, evidence of some terrible cruelty visited upon it. I knew that someone had given me the horse, but I hadn't wanted it, so I had left it in this paddock with plenty of grass and water.

The sky was darkening, and I encouraged the horse to take off and gallop to the far end of the paddock. As he picked up speed I saw that his coat was moth-eaten, and his welts and scars were weakening; and, as I watched, his belly opened up and all the liquefied innards spilled out, and the animal collapsed. I knew he was dying and wondered if I should ride the bike to get a vet; and I also knew I could do nothing for the animal, that horses die every day; and that I had to get to my appointment, even though I was still in my nightie, which might well catch in the wheels; and I got on the bike and rode away. I told myself again that it was not my fault.

As his ninetieth birthday approached, Dad refused to wash for twelve days straight. His wife decided it was time. She and her daughter and son-in-law found a bed in a nursing home in a faraway suburb, but Dad baulked at getting in the car. My older daughter was summoned: by some miracle she coaxed him and he followed her into her car and she drove him there. This was all conducted without my presence. I had no power, no influence, and no inclination to be involved.

I visited him the following day. He was the only patient in a double room, a tiny man in bed. His food was delivered and they sat him propped up at the edge of the mattress, his feet hanging over the side, but he would not eat. He had been washed and his hair had been cut, yet he was not shaven. That was too much, his wife told me. She was smoking a cigarette, against the rules, and she had the air of an elderly Marlene Dietrich, with a gravelly, accented voice. She had come for lunch, as they let spouses eat there, and she was complaining that he didn't want to sit in the dining room. She was acting like she'd made reservations in a fancy restaurant and the maître d' hadn't given them a table yet. Was she a little demented, too?

She showed me someone's Hawaiian shirt that had been mistakenly placed in Dad's cupboard. But anyway, she said, he doesn't care anymore.

The slippers fell off his feet and I saw that both of his big toes had grown inwards towards the other toes, so much so that they took a dive underneath them. I was shocked.

I didn't know he had such disfiguring bunions. I had small bunions. I knew bunions could be hereditary—did Mama also have bunions? I tried to visualise her feet but she'd died young, so maybe her bunions hadn't developed properly by then. Like her, they had run out of time.

Did Max have bunions? How common were they, anyway? Maybe I could go from bed to bed here and do a bunion survey?

I'd sometimes considered having an operation to straighten my toes, and this discovery settled it. I rang an orthopaedic surgeon who'd operated on me in the past and made an appointment. I would cut off my toes, like the girl in Hans Christian Andersen's 'The Red Shoes', in order not to be confused about who my father might be. After all this time I was not going to let a couple of stray digits undo all my good work.

My sister called to tell me that Dad was vomiting bile and seemed to be suffering from organ failure. His wife and her daughter had told the nursing home that they wanted him resuscitated under any circumstance, but they hadn't left formal instructions. His GP was away for the long weekend, and the nursing home couldn't contact his stepdaughter and her husband, the ones he trusted. He needed assessing, even if only for palliative medication, and the nursing-home people thought it best that an ambulance took him to the hospital. My sister knew about these things, so I left all this to her. What did I know of bile? More, in fact, than I would admit.

I met her at the emergency department and found Dad on a trolley, hooked up to a drip, in an immodest theatre gown. He was very distressed and they had to tape up the needle in his vein, as he kept trying to pull it out. The trolley had been lowered to the floor, to stop him from injuring himself as he threw the cotton blanket off and tried to leap over the edge. I kept covering him up, so firmly did I wish not to look upon his nakedness, and he kept trying to struggle with me. No, I told him. No, no, no. He insisted he was coming home with me. But you're not well, I said, and you are in hospital and they are helping you. He was wild-eyed, like a sick beast, like the horse in my dream.

I asked my sister to call the nurse. Give him something, I begged her, give him some Largactil. I remembered this from my days as a doctor's wife: that was what you gave belligerent, psychotic patients. A big fat injection was what I had in mind. They had already given him something, the nurse said. I was struggling with him over the blanket again. *Please give him more.* I felt like giving it to him myself. Or giving myself a big fat injection to take me away from there.

She explained that he'd had everything they could give him without it being dangerous. Dangerous? What was the danger in settling down a mad old dying man? Settling him right down in his grave.

I was more upset than I had been in years. It was horrible to be unable to calm him, without the power to remove him and not wanting him home with me. It was as if our whole relationship, stunted and hopeless, was being enacted in miniature in the little cubicle, its porous curtains unable to shield us.

Dad was returned to the nursing home without being admitted, as it was deemed the best place for him to die. Why he'd had to go on a nightmare ambulance ride and have me tussle with him at the hospital was beyond my understanding.

A phone call came in the morning from my older daughter to tell me that Dad had died. His stepdaughter and son-in-law made all the arrangements for the funeral. They had his power of attorney, and why not—he was closer to them than to us. I felt like I attended the funeral as a guest, except that I was sitting at the mourners' bench with my sister in the Orthodox Jewish cemetery, Dad's wife and stepdaughter sharing it with us.

Dad's son-in-law gave the eulogy. He read something biographical that my sister and I had written, as well as some of his own thoughts. He was moved to tears. I was not. I was feeling like a fraud there on the bench with my garment rent, as they say in the Torah. I was trying to remember Mama's funeral but it was so long ago and I was pregnant at the time and all I could recall was that I wore one of her woollen dresses on a cold and rainy October day. As usual, thoughts of her intruded upon this last opportunity for Dad to take centre stage.

We followed the simple pine coffin to the graveside and the rabbi said some prayers and I threw a handful of soil into the hole, as did others. The men took over the digging, and all I could think was that they should hurry up and fill it right to the top, so that he could never get out. I couldn't forget the terrible night of the hospital trolley and his animal panic to escape.

That night we gathered at my sister's house for the *minyan*. The men and women were in different parts of the house, but after the prayers we milled around and people shook our hands and told us how sorry they were. I was only sorry it hadn't come sooner. Dad's wife was smoking cigarettes and drinking tea, and I told her what a great job she had done looking after him and that we were grateful to her and that now she would be able to live her life with a bit more ease. And make new friends.

She told me she already had a friend, a man she had been meeting at the coffee shop where she went for years with Dad. They met each other every day at nine in the morning and parted at noon. Where did he go after that? Home to his wife, she said, who—of course—didn't understand him. I wondered if this woman was a serial understander of men whose wives didn't understand them.

My sister's eyebrows rose when I told her. How strange for my father's wife to be on the prowl on the very day he was buried. I tried to gather a bit of outrage or resentment, but it didn't feel right. Toes or not, I hardly had a leg to stand on.

Certified and apostilled

SHORTLY after Dad died, towards the end of the first decade of the new millennium, I was looking at a map showing projections of the world's climate with global warming taken into account. I saw that, according to one source, by 2050 Poland was going to be tropical and lush, while Australia would be hotter, drier and windier.

I thought about how my parents (whoever my father might have been) had made the decision to get on a boat and travel beyond the horizon to the bottom of the world, and of all the movements of history that had made them leave their Polish landscapes. They had been made stateless when Germany invaded Poland in 1939 and had remained so until they were permitted to take up Australian citizenship in 1955.

Mama had told me that before the war there had been a plan to go to Argentina, where part of her extended family had migrated, but the paperwork and permissions were too difficult and, besides, they couldn't get visas for the grandparents and they didn't want to leave the old ones behind. *Old ones.* I am probably older now than they were then.

Because of these stories, having all the correct documents was important to me. I always liked to apply early for whatever papers I needed. I was keen to make sure everything was in order, no slip-ups. *Alles in Ordnung.*

Mama and Dad's decision to get as far away from Europe as possible might well result in a hundred years of peace and prosperity for their children and their grandchildren. But their great-grandchildren, I suspected, might not thank them for having moved to the driest continent on a warming planet, especially if the place where they might have been born, had the path of history been otherwise, turned out to be paradise after all.

I wondered if it were possible to restore the family's citizenship rights in the country that might one day be a leafy tropical glade. I imagined acres of lush grasses and fruit trees and bison roaming the hills, which sat oddly alongside Dad's old stories of walking miles to school in snow and mud, wearing only thin garments. How would bison manage in the tropics with their woolly coats?

So began my long attempt to reclaim my Polish heritage, and to ensure that I could bestow it upon my grandchildren. I was sure I would be dead by 2050, but they might still have the chance to move to the northern hemisphere, if that was what they wanted.

It had been a longstanding family joke to rib me about my tendency to arrive early for everything, but the idea of my preparing for an event forty years hence that might not even happen would set a new, surely unsurpassable benchmark. I imagined my great-great-grandchildren being told of their eccentric but prescient foremother whose planning guaranteed their happy and comfortable lives.

Although Mama and Dad often spoke Polish to each other at home, and often within their circle of friends, they didn't teach me the language. What I picked up was mainly swear words or greetings. Their antipathy to Poland was understandable. One might avoid an enemy, Germany, but a former friend who had betrayed them, Poland, made them sadder and more hurt. Both Mama and Dad had been helped by Poles during the war, but these examples must have been outnumbered by those who were a threat to their lives. They had not been welcomed back to their homes when the war was over. They had escaped Poland because of the post-war murders of survivors by their former neighbours.

They had friends in Melbourne who did speak Polish to their children, so I'd heard a few more phrases to add to my meagre stockpile. There were those who spoke 'excellent Polish', which I knew meant they had no discernible Yiddish accent and they knew all the correct forms in the language, which has many cases and irregular rules and strict lines of formality. My parents had spoken only Yiddish till they were sent to school, so Polish was a second language for them, even though they were citizens of the country and their families had been living there for many centuries.

I could identify Polish when I heard it being spoken in the street or on SBS news. I could pick out a few words, and it sometimes made me nostalgic for a time when I heard Mama speaking the soft *sh*, *zh* and *ch* sounds. I could even parrot phrases well, but I couldn't understand what I was saying. It also made me anxious, though, precisely because

I didn't know what was being said. It confounded me to hear Polish spoken or to read it—it was both familiar and impenetrable, a sweet-sour state of confusion.

I started looking for online websites offering introductory Polish lessons. *Kawa* is the word for 'coffee'. That I knew, and it made sense—and this was only the first day. The internet course I chose was seductive, the little sound files instructive, and I immediately got going with a few familiar-sounding words: for 'film', 'gauze', 'garage' and 'hyena'.

The days of the month were poetic and descriptive: January was *Styczen*—from *stykać*, 'to bring into contact', when the old and new years join together; February was *Luty*, the word in Old Polish for 'bitter frost'; the spring of April was *Kwiecien*, from the word for 'flowers'; July was *Lipiec*, from *lipa*, the linden tree which flowered then; *Grudzien* was from *gruda*, the name for the cold, hard ground of December.

These were charming, and especially appealing to a lover of languages. But they made me nervous, too, as they were so different from the words I knew in English for the days and months. Nervous and curious. This was a good description of my general state.

I browsed online and learned that, at least according to Wikipedia, if you go to Poland as a Polish citizen and you don't have a Polish passport and travel instead on your Australian passport—well, this is illegal, and they won't let you out of the country unless you get a Polish passport, which another website said could take years to arrange. I panicked and thought about never going to Poland and avoiding the Polish authorities, with whom I could converse about a hyena being filmed in the garage but nothing much else. I felt I was stepping onto dangerous ground, *gruda*, cold and hard. Why was I wanting to send my poor little grandchildren to Poland?

Then, calming down, I remembered that they had parents, and no one knew what the politico-cultural climate would be after I was dead. Everything changes, sometimes even for the better. I would be giving them options. They were the ones who would have to work out which choices to make.

I found a local historian whose speciality was Polish–Jewish relations and Holocaust history, and whose parents were Polish Catholics. Her father was a World War II survivor who'd narrowly escaped the Katyn massacre of Polish army officers by the Soviets, and her great-uncle had been sent to Auschwitz for so-called collaboration. She ran a small business helping Jewish people to regain their Polish citizenship. This involved proving that at least one of your grandparents was Polish and thereby being able to stake a legitimate claim.

My mother's parents were both born in Poland. And probably both of my father's parents, too, but as I didn't know exactly who he was I decided to use whatever I could of the records available and hope that it would be enough to make my Polishness indisputable.

First, I had to answer a series of questions about my connection to Poland. Many people have tried to claim citizenship since Poland joined the European Union, often to further their chances of work, and the authorities would presumably be keen to see if I had a more honourable reason for my application.

I had to list all the usual things—my names, names of children, names of parents, names of grandparents, mother's siblings, father's siblings, towns of birth, last home address of people who lived in Poland—and if I'd ever visited Poland and knew anyone there. I'd met the former Polish ambassador to Australia, who helped me arrange some author interviews for my trip in the 1990s, so I mentioned her and the people I'd interviewed—the Nobel Prize-winning poet Czesław Miłosz, the novelist Tadeusz Konwicki and the literary editor Piotr Sommer—during that visit. I thought that this would seem impressive.

What did the family do before the war? Occupations, home addresses, and what happened to them during the Nazi occupation? When did my parents leave Poland? Who was left behind? Where did my parents go after leaving? Dates, places? What did they do in Australia, and where did they live? When did they die? Were they naturalised? Did my father serve in any army? Is there any family alive in Poland today? Many of the answers to these questions were 'no', 'none', 'nobody' and 'don't know'.

There were documents to be found, scanned, translated, certified and apostilled: certificates of birth, death, marriage and changes of name. Archival records from Poland: registration of addresses, school reports, old passports, documents from Mama and Dad's stay in the Displaced Persons camp in Germany after the war.

There were some records available in the National Archives of Australia—migration documents, incoming-passenger cards, boat-arrival lists, naturalisation certifi-cates—but the rest of the tasks seemed impossibly onerous given the time since my mother's death, and the burning of the families and their histories in the cauldron of war. The application process appeared to be designed to evoke defeat-ism in the face of massive concrete Soviet-style bureaucracy.

It seemed unjust, but I was determined to succeed. I rolled up my sleeves. It was an irresistible demand, one that required a bold response.

I started with the National Archives in Canberra. There were records of Dad's arrival: *Hryniewiecki, Aron Lejzor—Nationality: Polish—Arrived Melbourne per Caboto 28 October 1949.* Mama was there, too: *Sara, nee Kawer.*

I imagined them arriving on the dock at Port Melbourne. Mama had told me that Dad bought a second-hand wicker suitcase in Paris before they left, and it had fallen apart on the dock when they disembarked. She was humiliated: strangers had to help her collect all her clothes and person-al belongings from the ground. Dad remembered going to the beach on Melbourne Cup day four days later and getting badly sunburnt. This was the sort of thing I knew about them. I doubted if the Polish authorities would find these stories sufficient.

I became a denizen of the Victorian Registry of Births, Deaths and Marriages, going to the office for copies of certificates and then for new copies when the copies I'd sent on had been misplaced. It seemed that almost no document was sufficient in itself. Each had to be further stamped and guaranteed. I had to get documents apostilled at the Depart-ment of Foreign Affairs. I had to have a document sworn by a notary. I'd had no previous experience with apostilles and notaries, but I became adept at queuing and applying and paying and collecting.

I knew of no formal change-of-name document for my parents. They'd changed their last name from Hryniewiecki by selecting five consecutive letters from the Polish name and seemed not to have formally told anyone. Later, I found a 1950 letter in the National Archives from an agent of the Commonwealth Migration Officer to a solicitor, advising that

> under existing Departmental ruling it is not permis-
> sible for an alien, residing in Australia, to adopt a
> name in an accepted Anglicised form. As the name
> Ryon is, phonetically, of this type I regret to inform
> you that approval for the proposed change of name
> cannot be granted.

So they were stymied by bureaucrats suspicious of the motives of these aliens trying to pass themselves off as Irish, albeit with a crazy spelling which would have had its own annoying consequences had they been able to go ahead.

There was no register of their formal marriage, save for the unfilled-in form with their signatures that I'd unearthed on my trip to Poland years earlier. But my sister remem-bered that there must have been a record for their Jewish marriage, in order for us to have been married in Orthodox synagogues. I discovered there'd been a fire in the records office of the synagogue I was married in, and there was nothing in the way of official Jewish divorce documents either. Then I remembered that I'd supervised my parents' divorce, which was a rush job in the months before Mama died in 1977, and straight away I chased down the lawyer who helped us. I recalled how he'd come down to the car, which I'd parked in a no-standing zone in the centre of the city, outside his office. He needed my mother's signature but she was too weak to come up to his office.

The lawyer agreed that the original marriage certificate may well have been in the divorce application. He applied to the Family Court archives and they released the official *ksuba*, a statement handwritten in Aramaic on a thin and yellowed sheet of paper. It had been drawn up in Siedlce by one of the other survivors, and it had served as the official Jewish marriage certificate when Dad made himself a wedding suit and a dress out of pink paper for Mama.

The application for our family's Polish passports became a kind of hobby for me. I had to write to the Repki local government office near my mother's birthplace, Wyrozęby, for a copy of her birth certificate. I had been there myself in 1996 and had discovered that much of the archive was destroyed in the war. They gave me a new certificate based on information she'd given them when she returned from her undercover time in Warsaw. She was trying to marry Dad so they could leave Poland, but at seventeen she was legally underage. Technically, she needed permission from a guardian, but all of her guardians were dead. I imagine this might have resulted in a protracted legal story, and I knew they were in a hurry to flee. I was given a copy of a birth certificate that listed her birth date as being four years earlier than it really was. I knew it was wrong. But it was official, and what was more wrong—the unofficial truth or an official lie?

I signed the letter that my historian accomplice wrote to the Siedlce civil office. The records of Dad's birth and his parents' marriage did not exist anymore. She asked them about my report of the incomplete marriage certificate with my parents' signatures on it. They wouldn't tell her anything over the phone. I didn't blame them—it sounded crazy to me, too, and I'd seen the certificate being dug out of the 'unfiled documents' folder with my own eyes.

We sent all our Australian passports to the Polish consulate in Sydney. They sent them back in our self-addressed envelopes. We had the sense that finally progress was being made.

I had to apply for a change of details to my Australian birth certificate, as it had a misspelled version of my mother's place of birth and Dad's name, and had not mentioned the town where he was born. Up till then, I hadn't noticed. But the Polish authorities were on to even the most minor mistake, and these were rather major. And they didn't like staples and they didn't like blue ink.

By the beginning of the following year, many months later, we all had our Polish citizenship documents. I looked at the papers that had been sent to my house, and among the mostly incomprehensible Polish phrases there were our names and dates of birth and official numbers and an official stamp.

For the children, the next step was to register their Australian birth and marriage certificates in Poland, and then to apply for a special number—a PESEL—and for passports. For me, the road ahead was potholed and circuitous.

I'd been divorced and had changed my married name

by deed poll, taking the Polish 'w' out of it and putting in a streamlined 'v'. This made it easier for people to pronounce: as I worked in radio, there were a lot of pronunciations each day that could go wrong. I thought this was a good idea at the time, but it now proved costly.

In the past I'd been summoned to the Family Court. My ex-husband had got annoyed when people—dentists, school administrators, parents of my children's friends—occasionally made the mistake of spelling our children's last name with a 'v' rather than a 'w'. He wrongly assumed that this was done on purpose—engineered by me—to usurp him. And he engaged a barrister to take me to court.

The judge was confused. He pointed out that I could not be held responsible for the spelling mistakes of the rest of the world, and dismissed the claim. My ex had spent a lot of money on legal advice and was furious. The case of the Vs and the Ws was a funny story I told for years afterwards... and then it came back to haunt me.

Unlike the relative ease of registering my Australian birth and marriage certificates in Poland, I needed to have my Australian divorce recognised by a Polish court. I suspected this might be because post-Soviet Poland was reverting to a Catholic approach, and divorce was in a special legal category again. The bureaucracy, though, retained a distinctly Soviet flavour.

I needed to find a lawyer in Warsaw, and neither my contacts nor the Polish consulate could help me. I visited yet another office to get a copy of my divorce decree and took it to the Department of Foreign Affairs for an apostille. I was getting very good at this.

I wrote to lawyers whose names came up on a Google search, and judged them by their English responses and whether they got back to me at all. Once I settled on one I began explaining my situation. All I wanted was for my divorce to be confirmed and the documents to be registered in the name I'd used for thirty years. A name that I'd changed by deed poll. A name that had caused me some aggravation with my ex-husband.

The divorce document could be registered in time, came the reply. But I would have to get my ex-husband's agreement that I could use my name spelt with a 'v', and he had to confirm that he was aware that we were indeed divorced. I'd not asked him for anything in three decades, and now this—the Vs and the Ws again raising their ugly heads. I was gutted.

I waited for his consent letter to arrive by post, but it seemed he'd asked a friend who spoke Polish to check that what he was signing was correct. I wondered why he couldn't use Google Translate—that was what I'd been using for months—but I resisted the urge to hurry him up.

Soon I was to travel overseas for work. I desperately wanted to post the document before I left. The night before we were due to go I covered the kitchen table with attempts at copying his signature. Some I imagined were rather good, but I then thought better of it. I left the country without the signature.

When I got back, there in the letterbox was the envelope with my ex-husband's familiar writing on it. It must have come the day I had left and before the post was due to be held at the post office. To my dismay, snails had eaten their way around the envelope. When I opened it, I saw with relief that the signature was intact. But the page looked like an attempt by a school child to reproduce a ye-olde-worlde treasure map.

Still, here it was, and I was not going to ask for another. I sent it to Warsaw.

I learned some months later that the judge thought the document was a forgery. So I needed to ask for another original and to get it signed by a notary as a witness, and get a red wax seal on it, too. By now I was used to this. Rather than give up, I did as I was instructed.

By the end of the year my divorce document had arrived. I was now officially divorced in Poland, more than thirty years after I achieved that status in Australia. My ex-husband kindly didn't mention the case of the Vs and the Ws. Until his signed document had been accepted by another bureau-crat in a Warsaw office, my Polish passport in the correct name remained out of reach. I was getting worried that by the time I could apply there would be a language test, and maybe a test in astronomy too, as a nod to Copernicus. I had to ask myself why I was pursuing this task with such vigour. Seeking a Polish passport seemed like yet another attempt to claim authenticity, to get the right papers, to restore something that was lost.

I'd thought I was doing it for the grandchildren— but they were Polish now and had the passports to prove it, with their identities and options in the hands of their parents. Whereas I was trapped in a web of legal intrigue to get my passport, and I didn't even know why it mat-tered so much to me. Or even if it mattered at all, and had instead become a kind of game, or a kind of tic.

A passport was evidence of legitimacy as a citizen. But I had an Australian passport and Australian citizenship. I was a legitimate citizen of this country. The Polish passport might be speaking to something deeper, a confirmation of where my parents came from and that I had a stake in the place. My 1997 radio documentary made after the Polish trip was partly about looking for a hole in the ground where Dad had hidden. It was like looking for an empty grave, a man-shaped hole in the ground. The search for my father had brought me to a question mark, a space that contained nothing.

Three years after I began this particular quest for an identity, I received the document from the Polish Consulate that officially changed my name from Kowal to Koval and opened the way for me to get a Polish passport. The next step was to go to Sydney with all my documents and apply. And then the passport would come, and then I would think about what it meant and why it had been such a drawn-out affair.

Waiting for the plane to Sydney I was anxious: about missing the flight, or finding the consulate closed when I got there, even though I'd called the week before to check that it would be open. I was anxious about discovering that I needed yet another document, or that my photographs were no longer the right size, or that I didn't have enough cash. Or that I needed to speak fluent Polish to apply. Or that all of the rules had changed. It was like an anxiety dream, a Kafka story.

It always felt dangerous interacting with the consulate,

dealing with a vast bureaucracy and suspecting that there were secret reasons for its reticence to accept me. I'd recently seen a news report about a move to outlaw ritual slaughter in Poland—the last time that a law like this was proposed was the mid-1930s, something about banning the production of kosher food.

It was upsetting. Not that I was dependent on kosher food, but I was alarmed at the idea that there were people who might want to ban it. But then I reasoned that if all the idiotic ideas of Australia's fringe politicians were publicised overseas it would reflect poorly on this country, even if they weren't representative of our collective thinking.

There were more troubling questions. Why did I want legitimacy from the government of a country that my parents fled? They were so damaged by their experiences there that they didn't teach me Polish. But it was a language that I heard each day in the house. Maybe I wanted to restore certain memories or gain information about what they might have been talking or fighting about.

And there was my anxiety about needing the correct papers. About Mama's forged papers being the secret to her survival. I couldn't avoid seeing the connection.

I wanted the Polish passport, but was torn between using it and not using it. I was unsure about what would happen if I got into difficulties somewhere in the world and needed diplomatic support. If I couldn't speak the language, what would happen—though what could I possibly do that would require the diplomatic support of the Polish government?

Kafka's Josef K. didn't know what he had done in *The Trial*, but he was still in trouble. As a young reader I had identified with him. I must have thought there was something about me that was different, questionable, illegitimate, without being sure what it was.

I thought about my husband's attempts before the trip to calm me down. He quizzed me about Poland, in case they asked me questions when I was there. What's the epic poem of Polish culture? *Pan Tadeusz* by Adam Mickiewicz. I knew that. He asked what it's about and I didn't know, so we googled late into the night. Mistaken identity, lost Polish pride, lost loves, complex misunderstandings, a girl called Zosia. Right.

And who's the prime minister of Poland? Donald Tusk. What kind of a name is Donald for a Pole? Tusk is from the Kashubian minority, which in the car to the airport I could only remember as Kardashian. It's pronounced *Toosk*, according to Wikipedia. The title of Poland's national anthem translates as 'Poland is not yet lost'. Would they test me?

At the consulate in Sydney a woman who I thought might be the consul—dark-haired, forty-five, neat-figured— greeted me. She seemed to be temporarily staffing the desk.

I said, 'I have to apply for my Polish passport.'

She said, 'You have to?'

I said, 'I wish to—I'm here to.'

I smiled. She didn't.

She asked if I had my documents, yes; my photograph, yes; my Australian passport for identification, yes. She checked them. I held my breath. They are all in order, she said, and handed me two forms to fill in. She pointed out where to sign, *here* and *here*, and to start with questions one to twenty. They were all in Polish. She offered no help, even though I had conducted the whole conversation in English, apart from my hello. She motioned to a table for me to sit down with the forms and asked the next person in line to step up.

I fired up my Google Translate app, and when others who spoke Polish sat down at the table I asked discreetly for confirmation that this or that line was correct. One woman obliged but I felt she was unwilling. Another woman who learned Polish as a child but who couldn't read very well was more co-operative.

After an hour the consul asked me how I was going. I brought the forms to her, a child handing in homework to the teacher. She used white-out to obliterate some of my answers. She told me that in response to the question about the colour of my eyes I must not write 'blue', but the Polish word for it. Fair enough.

I returned to the desk feeling like I was in the remedial class at school. I was never in any remedial class. The word for 'blue' is *niebieskie*.

In the nationality box I wrote 'Polski' over the whited-out 'Australian and Polish'. When I returned to the desk the consul pronounced the forms correct, except for a missing 'e'.

'Ah, *Polskie*,' I said, 'because I am a woman.'

She neither confirmed nor denied this.

I began to feel relieved as she took copies of my documents. The computer system was down, she said, but she could do it by hand. If there were any problems with my papers, they would contact me. I told her I was from Melbourne and it would be hard for me to return. She was unmoved.

The consul took fingerprints of my index fingers, and I handed her $152 in cash. She apologised that the process had taken me an hour and a half. (Years, I thought, not hours.) But I could have closed the consulate, as the computers are down, she repeated. I agreed that it was better that she hadn't. I farewelled her in Polish, went outside and looked for a cab.

As soon as I got in, the driver asked me if I knew what year the Japanese submarines entered Sydney Harbour. I can't remember, I said. I'm from Melbourne. This was an odd answer. But it was the one I gave to the Polish consulate as well. I wondered if I seemed illegitimate to the taxi driver, too.

He'd trained as an electronic engineer, but when he got to Australia in 1989 his English wasn't good enough for him to work; and then, when it was better, electronic engineering had moved on. He spoke and read Chinese and Japanese. He wanted to write his life story but thought it was too late. He worked twelve hours a day, seven days a week. He had no friends. He was lonely. But he read.

When I arrived at the airport I had a headache. Too many stories of displacement, too many languages for one day.

16

The longest journey

THERE was no way to avoid it, no matter how hard I tried. I had to piece together what might have happened to Max in Auschwitz, and what brought him to the moment when he may or may not have become my biological father. At first I'd had an interest in who he was and what parts of him might have been transmitted to me, but after following his story for years I'd become interested in filling in all the gaps that I could, not just for personal reasons but for the sake of the story itself. I had become immersed in its meanderings and sharp corners, and found myself swept up in it. I was intrigued by the tributaries of Max's story, too, the way the stories of others overlapped with it.

Alongside my quest for the right Polish documents, I was studying the Auschwitz video testimonies and reading Holocaust literature. I'd do this during the day and then take sleeping tablets each night to knock me out. If I didn't take the pills, the phrases and terrible scenes would play in my mind when my head hit the pillow and I wouldn't find the sweet place where sleep was possible.

I knew I was no historian, but it seemed logical to me

that these men with whom Max had entered the camp and with whom he had been tattooed, with whom he survived and with whom he joined to travel to Germany to testify against Paulikat, would have shared with him some other critical experiences. Their stories must have intersected in some way. I might learn from their analyses what made one man live and the man next to him die—apart from luck, which wasn't something you could influence.

From the testimonies I'd watched I knew that those who were strong to begin with, or used to the cold, or used to hard regimes, or able to 'organise' better food or a better position in the bunks away from the reach of bashing Kapos and not too high near the roof so as to choke from lack of air, or had tradeable goods or skills, or had a knowledge of how things worked and who to bribe and who to trust—such attributes gave prisoners an advantage and made it possible to still be breathing, albeit in a skeletal and diseased shell of a body, when the war was finally over.

I read through books on my shelves till I came to one bought years before: Hermann Langbein's *People in Auschwitz*, an account of life in the camp written by an Austrian political prisoner. He'd been arrested for being a Communist activist. His positions in the camp, as an office worker in the infirmary and a member of the underground resistance, gave him a point of view that I found fresh and compelling.

I'd avoided reading his book because the title and cover seemed to promise great distress, but by the time I opened its covers I thought I might have become inured to nightmare visions through reading the works of Eli Wiesel and Primo Levi (who, like Max, had also worked in the

Auschwitz infirmary) and, more recently, Robert Antelme. Though Langbein's outlook and language were calm and penetrating, still the night terrors came.

After spending three days reading the book I was relieved to have completed it. I had a palpitating heart and couldn't catch my breath. This was anxiety, my old friend, yet here I was in my home, at my desk, no crematoria in sight but in my mind's eye.

And now I wanted Hermann Langbein to be my father. He was born in Vienna in 1912, two years before Max, to a middle-class family. His mother was Catholic and his father a Protestant convert from Judaism. He trained and worked as an actor before being an organiser for the Communist Party. After the annexation of Austria by Germany in 1938 he fled first to Switzerland, then to France and finally to Spain, where he joined the International Brigade to fight against Franco in the Civil War. When it ended he was interned with other members of the brigade in various French camps. Following the German conquest, the Vichy regime handed them to the Germans and Langbein was transferred to Dachau, then in 1942 to Auschwitz, where he remained for two years.

As an Austrian interned for his activism he was given a privileged job as clerk to the chief SS physician in the infirmary, and from his position in that circle of hell he could both witness and document events. His number was 60355, so he had arrived before Max, but not long before.

When he was liberated, Langbein became general secretary of the Comité International des Camps and set about not only analysing what he had seen but reading all the other available survivor and witness testimonies. He started campaigning to bring some of the perpetrators to justice—such as it was in post-war Germany. He filed accusations against Carl Clauberg, who had conducted sterilisation experiments in Auschwitz; he filed accusations against Josef Mengele, who fled to Argentina before he could be extradited; he filed accusations against Wilhelm Boger, which led to the first big Auschwitz trial, in Frankfurt in 1963. He attended most court sessions and published a documentary account of the trial shortly after the verdicts came down.

As was the case with Robert Antelme, being a political prisoner gave Langbein a more protected life in the camp. More than that, his sober understanding of the human condition, perhaps because he was already mature when he was interned, made him a contemporary Virgil for me.

From Langbein I learned that Max was well placed to be given a work detail on his arrival in Auschwitz, being twenty-eight in 1942, tall, strong and a tailor, one of the trades needed for factory work in the camp. Langbein quotes Primo Levi, from *Survival in Auschwitz*:

> At Auschwitz, in 1944, of the old Jewish prisoners
> (we will not speak of the others here, as their condi-
> tion was different), '*kleine Nummer*', low numbers less
> than 150,000, only a few hundred had survived; not one
> was an ordinary Häftling, vegetating in the ordinary
> Kommandos, and subsisting on the normal ration.
> There remained only the doctors, tailors, shoemak-
> ers, musicians, cooks, young attractive homosexuals,
> friends or compatriots of some authority in the camp;

or they were particularly pitiless, vigorous, and
inhuman individuals, installed (following an investi-
ture by the SS command, which showed itself in such
choices to possess satanic knowledge of human beings)
in the posts of Kapos, *Blockältester*, etc.; or finally, those
who, without fulfilling particular functions, had
always succeeded through their astuteness and energy
in successfully organizing, gaining in this way, besides
material advantages and reputation, the indulgence and
esteem of the powerful people in the camp. Whosoever
does not know how to become an 'Organisator,' 'Kombi-
nator,' 'Prominent' (the savage eloquence of these
words!) soon become a 'musselman'...They followed
the slope down to the bottom, like streams that run
down to the sea.

And in *The Drowned and the Saved*, Levi elaborates:

Unlike the purely persecutory labour...work could
instead at times become a defense. It was so for the
few in the Lager who were made to exercise their
own trade: tailors, cobblers, carpenters, blacksmiths,
bricklayers; such people, resuming their customary
activity, recover at the same time, to some extent,
their human dignity.

Tailors made uniforms for the Wehrmacht and the SS, including specialist riding breeches, as well as civilian clothes.
The factory offered an opportunity to mix with Polish
workers from outside the camp, and this meant a chance
to trade. Langbein details the underground economy, the

possibility that if you had a connection in 'Canada' there might be a chance of obtaining a watch or a piece of jewellery which could be bartered for food on the outside.

A few eggs or butter that had been exchanged for a diamond would not be consumed by the ravenous black marketeer but rather be traded with people who worked in the bakery for loaves of bread. The bread would be divided among all who'd taken part in the process. Every step, every transaction came with the risk of death, and many unlucky traders were executed.

I knew from Alan that Max had said he'd managed to get a better job in the infirmary. But what was a tailor doing there? I discovered that SS medics who assisted in the infirmary didn't have to be trained, and in Aleksander Lasik's account in *Anatomy of the Auschwitz Death Camp* they were often cobblers, tailors and farmers.

My Virgil, Hermann Langbein, wrote that the infirmary was a desirable posting, despite the possibility of contracting contagious diseases, as it provided a roof over your head, you were excused from violent roll calls, and there was more to eat, because

> there were always patients with no appetite and dead people whose rations could still be obtained, since they were prudently not reported as having died until the number of required meals had been submitted. Finally, members of this detail belonged to the upper stratum of camp society, for experienced inmates fostered friendships with HKB [infirmary] personnel.

Max worked first as a tailor and then in the infirmary, a step up. His younger nephew told me some years after we first met that Max's brother-in-law had been a Kapo in the camp. I thought this connection might have been how Max got a better job, and been the source of rumours about him. No wonder he was proud of his number, a signal to himself and others that here was a strong man, a clever man, a cunning man, a lucky man, and perhaps a man not to be trifled with.

An email arrived from an academic I'd written to in the law faculty at the University of Amsterdam who had an interest in war-crimes trials.

> Dear Ms Koval,
> Max Dunne is named as a witness in a judgment
> relating to a killing in Striegenau, Poland (see case no.
> 755: http://www1.jur.uva.nl/junsv/brd/Tatortengfr.
> htm). He may well have testified in other cases as well,
> but as his testimony was not explicitly included in
> the judgments of these cases, we have no knowledge
> about that. This can only be established by checking
> the files of the relevant Auschwitz cases, but you might
> also inquire with the Zentrale Stelle in Ludwigsburg.
> Perhaps they know. The files of the Striegenau case
> (including Dunne's testimony) are either at the
> State Attorney's Office (Staatsanwaltschaft) with the
> Landgericht Arnsberg (judgment of the 23 June 1971;
> file number: 6 Ks 3/70), or at a state archive to which
> the people at the Staatsanwaltschaft will, no doubt,
> be able to point you. You can find the address of the

Staatsanwaltschaft by means of googling the Land-
gericht. Good luck with your search!
Yours sincerely,
Dick de Mildt

I did as he suggested and, in the halting German I'd learned
in the two months at the Goethe-Institut in Berlin, I wrote
to the Staatsanwaltschaft in Arnsberg for a copy of Max's
testimony.

While I waited I read *Rodinsky's Room*, by Rachel Lichtenstein and Iain Sinclair, about the search for a man who disappeared from his room above the Princelet Street Synagogue
in Spitalfields, London in 1969 and was never heard of again.
David Rodinsky's room was opened up a decade after his
disappearance, and since then people had been going
through the mess and books and his notes, trying to work
out who he was and what might have happened to him.

Like my project, it too was a quest, and I could see the
romantic projections that Lichtenstein made as she travelled
all over the world following up clues in the cabbalistic notes
of her quarry. I had to examine myself for signs of romanti-
cism. There didn't seem to be, on the surface at least, much
romance in finding the truth of Max's story and the way it
might have intersected with mine. Max Dunne sounded
like an angry, damaged man, even if it was clear to me why
he might have become like that.

I combed through Auschwitz literature to find out
more about the jobs that were regarded as 'good' in the
camp. What went on in the infirmary? How romantic could
I be with this material that I had to work with?

Rachel Lichtenstein had far more to go on than I did. She had photographs and documents and other people's memories. And she could make contact with people and ask them anything she liked without feeling as if she was going to open old wounds or embarrass them or shock them with her very existence.

Then an envelope from Germany arrived in the post. I was renting a shared writing room in an old mansion near my house and my writer roommate, a German speaker, happily agreed to help me with the translation. We headed to our local coffee shop. I was excited, as I expected to 'hear' the voice of my father for the first time. Though not the voice of a father reading a little girl bedtime stories or praising her school results or warning her tenderly about the ways of the world.

It would be the voice of a former Auschwitz inmate who had been damaged by terrible experiences, who had lost most of his family and who was probably under great stress, standing in a German courthouse twenty-five years after his liberation, giving evidence in a war-crimes trial. It was not a transcript of every one of the words he spoke, but a deposition of his evidence. It had been given in his recently acquired English (did he speak with a strong accent, did he hesitate?) and translated into German at the time. And I was attempting a translation back to English, more than forty years later. What voice could I really expect to hear?

The date of the testimony was 21 October 1970. I was finishing Year Eleven at that time.

First, Max confirmed his identity through his Australian passport: G262151.

He described himself as a manufacturer and designer. He was fifty-six years old and living in Melbourne, Australia—he was younger then than I was now, I realised. Max told the court:

> I was born on 23 December 1914 in Mława. I went to the government school in Mława and later to a school for design in Warsaw. Afterwards I came back to Mława. Then the war broke out. I was not yet married. My brother went to Australia in 1937. I moved to the ghetto in Mława at the beginning of 1941 with my parents and was there till 16 November 1942 when we were deported to Auschwitz with the second transport.

Max testified that he was present at mass hangings and shootings on particular days in the ghetto. He described how people looked, estimating their heights and remembering details of what they were wearing and who else was there:

> A lieutenant of the *Schutzpolizei* [security police] from Mława, I can't remember his name at the moment, but it may come to me. I remember him especially because his girlfriend Marysia Wrablowska went to school with me. He was good-looking, about thirty-eight years old... he was six feet tall, with middle-blond hair. There were also others there.
> A man called Paulikat.
> He had a light-green uniform on and was a member of the gendarmerie. He was as far as I know an under-officer. He was very good-looking, with a round face and about six feet tall. As I heard it he had lost his

finger when he had taken part in the Spanish Civil War.

At the hanging there was also a member of the security police from Mława called Fost. He was very tall, more than six feet, maybe in his middle-thirties, he wore a dark-green uniform and a round SS insignia on his jacket.

There was also a *Schutzpolizei* called Blum who was thirty-five years old and five feet eight inches tall.

From his descriptions I imagined that Max had a designer's eye for detail and a tailor's sense of bodily proportions. I caught myself thinking that I may have inherited his eye for detail.

I remembered a joke Dad told about a tailor. Why was I thinking about the joke now? I was assuming that Max was a better tailor than Dad. I wanted him to be.

Dad's joke was about a man who went to his tailor to be fitted for a new suit. When he put on the coat he saw it was longer on one side. He complained, and the tailor said it was because the man was standing crooked and if he would just raise one shoulder the suit would fit fine. Same story with one of the pants legs. (You really need to see me when I tell this joke, as it has a physical punch line.)

When the man with the new suit was walking crookedly along the street with his shoulder and leg adjusted as the tailor required, he was spied by another man across the road who whispered to his wife, 'I must find out who made that man's suit,' and the wife said, 'Why do you want to know?' and the husband said: 'Because if that tailor could make such a nice suit for a cripple like him, imagine what he could do for a normal man!'

When Dad occasionally made a coat for me when I was young he would say that the coat fitted well but that I was standing crookedly, so it didn't look quite right. The coat Dad made me was wrong because I was wrong.

And that is why I was combing a translated war-crimes testimony for things I might be proud of in the man who may or may not have been my father; who may or may not have been a damaged, difficult man; who may or may not have even cared if I was dead or alive. And part of me was stretching out the experience of hearing the transcript, as I could see it was only a page or two and this was almost certainly the first and last time I'd be able to read something that resembled a direct address by Max.

He was talking about what had happened in the past and, although he did not know it then, he was addressing himself to the future, to me (whoever I was to him), sitting with my friend in a coffee shop more than four decades later:

> I knew all the murdered people, as they were from Mława. At the moment I can only remember a few names of the seventeen—Samuel Korzenik, Chaim Solarski.
>
> In autumn 1942, it was two months before the deportation to Auschwitz, it was in September, when hundreds of young men, including myself, were arbitrarily singled out by the Mława security police.
>
> We had to line up in the square of the ghetto. I remember distinctly that Fost was there. I believe that Paulikat was also there. When we were taken to a house in the ghetto I managed to run away. The remainder were held under arrest for a week. The guards had

the house surrounded. Another person was probably arrested in my place.

Max managed to run away. He knew that this meant that another young man was arrested in his place. The moral code of the camps and the ghettos was beginning to take hold of him.

He also tells the court that someone else was probably killed because he'd taken the chance to escape. He didn't have to say it. But it was on his mind after everything he had experienced.

[F]our hundred young men were all shot. The entire ghetto population was ordered to be present at the shooting. I saw with my own eyes that Fost and Paulikat took part in the shooting. All the security police with reinforcement from nearby locations formed the firing squad. The shooting lasted several hours.

At the beginning of 1942 a woman named Pultusk-ier was shot by Fost on the street. I came a few minutes afterward to see the corpse of the woman lying in the street. I heard that Fost had shot the woman. The reason for the shooting I don't know, it was maybe because she had with her some bread or milk. He did it just for fun. He was a beast.

By then, Max must have known bestiality when he saw it. I respected his judgement.

In 1942, the exact date I can't remember, Mr Perlmutter from the ghetto elders committee was called to the

guard police outside the ghetto and there he was
shot by Fost. It was Fost that shot him. It was told
to me by Wengelein's chauffeur who is now a taxi
driver in Mława who I spoke with when I visited
there in June 1967. I don't know why Perlmutter
was shot. The name of the lieutenant which I
have just remembered was Wengelein.

So Max had gone back to Mława in 1967. Although Alan had
said Max had been back to Auschwitz, I hadn't known that
he went back to his hometown, too. It was very early to be
making the trip back, at a time when Poland was behind the
Iron Curtain. I wondered if he was researching his testimony, collecting his wits, reliving his time there.

Maybe if he hadn't had to be a tailor or a manufacturer or a designer or whatever he thought of himself as,
he would have been a thorough researcher. I was happy to
see he'd remembered the name of the lieutenant that had
earlier escaped him. I silently cheered him. I was becoming
attached to Max, or at least to his account of himself.

Our transport to Auschwitz was under the
command of the accused. We had to go three
kilometres from the ghetto to the railway station.
That was the longest journey of my life.
　　It was already very cold.
　　The accused was present on the march.
　　He supervised the transport from the ghetto
to the station.
　　Ten people lay dead who couldn't manage
this three-kilometre journey.

Those who couldn't continue were shot.
Who shot them, I couldn't today say.
I don't know any more today if Wengelein
was there, but I am sure that the accused was.
The people were hopeless and dejected.
I don't know if the accused had a dog with
him, I had to take care of my relatives.

That was the longest journey of his life, he said. He had to take care of his relatives.

He cared for his relatives, for everyone. Everyone, that is, but me.

17

How do I look?
What do they think?

LET'S leave Max there, on the longest journey of his life, from the ghetto in Mława in that cold winter of 1942 to the train station. His life in a new kind of hell is about to begin—and you may well be thinking that I am being whiny and unreasonable in writing, 'Everyone, that is, but me.'

I've tried to look at things from the point of view of an adult who is piecing together the story of her life from scraps, from whispers here and there, from veiled comments, from the unreliable recollections of people who might be ill or traumatised or have little direct experience or knowledge of the things that I wanted to tell. What can I say in my defence? (Why have I put myself on trial here?)

It was just a small cry from a little girl who was overlooked, ignored, passed over. What about me, Daddy?

I may not have the right to ask that question. But to whom should I be directing it?

Mama, what about me?

In my pursuit of Max, I had taken my eyes off another

player in the drama. And while I was waiting for Max's testimony to arrive and searching through Holocaust stories, I came upon interviews with people who had survived using false identities, as Mama did in Warsaw.

What did I really know of her story? I knew what she had let slip, augmented by things I had learned since her death. She said she had fair hair and blue eyes, and she had been chosen by her mother as the one most likely to be able to pass for a Polish Catholic girl. Her fifteen-year-old brother had dark hair and brown eyes. According to a story Bern told me, on the night before the ghetto was to be 'liquidated' and all the inmates sent to their deaths at Treblinka my grandmother gave her daughter a potato, the last of their food. She told Mama that where they were going they would have no need to eat.

When I visited the hamlet of Wyrozęby during my trip to Poland I learned that two of Mama's neighbours, brother and sister Joseph and Josepha Krzyzanowski, still lived across the road from her old house in a small wooden cottage in which a tap had just been connected after two hundred years of having to draw water from a well. They remembered Mama, were surprised that she had survived the war. 'She disappeared like camphor,' Joseph told me. They said that a woman named Wanda Bujalska, a member of a minor Polish aristocratic family who were local landowners in the region where Mama's family had a small farm holding, was most likely the one who had arranged Mama's false identity papers.

I found the Bujalska house high on a hill overlooking the valley; by then it had been turned into a school, but it was summer and the place was deserted. I sat in the garden in the shade of birch and poplars and fragrant Polish jasmine, imagining the secret visits here of underground couriers as the plans for Mama's false documents were hatched.

Recently I found a reference to Wanda Bujalska in a weekly paper published in Sokołów Podlaski. It was an interview with her nephew about his recollection of wartime activities in the local district. After the death of her husband in 1927 in Wyrozęby, Wanda Bujalska rarely mixed with the locals. She was highly educated and had a circle of worldly artists—actors, popular singers, opera stars; names which are still recognised in Poland: Nina Andrycz, Janusz Popławski, Mieczysław Fogg. Fogg was a member of the Polish underground.

Members of the underground visited Wanda Bujalska in her house, and it was there that she hid several Jews from Warsaw through the war. When it was all over, she lost control of the estate to another family member and a group of survivors organised for her to stay in a flat in Warsaw, to repay her. I see she died in the city in 1976, aged eighty-six.

Most likely Wanda Bujalska had given Mama contacts in Warsaw, and Mama slipped out of view to walk by herself, a fourteen-year-old girl, the nearly one hundred kilometres to Warsaw to find shelter with a Polish family. They had agreed to put her up; she paid someone for the false identity papers with a small blue-stoned ring that her mother had given her; and she lived in the basement of their home, looking after Rolf, their large German shepherd, and learning to be a Catholic—how to pray properly and what was expected of her in church.

She was from a rural Orthodox Jewish family: her first

language was Yiddish and she'd learned Polish at the village school. Suddenly she was living in a sophisticated metropolis, using her second language, and she was barely a teenager. Her papers said that she was seven years older than she was.

I knew that after Mama had spent about six months in the Warsaw basement, one of the family members, a brother-in-law or son-in-law who was a journalist, became rattled by the possibility that they would be discovered hiding a Jewish girl, and Mama had to leave. Where she went after that, how she disappeared as a young teenager into the Nazi-occupied city, is a mystery, but I knew that somehow she got a job as a waitress in a canteen for German soldiers.

Just as I had pursued Max by tracking the group of men who testified with him and who were tattooed in the same transport arrival from Mława, I searched for stories like Mama's.

I was trying to understand how it was possible for her to live her life in Australia in the 1950s, with children from two different fathers, and how she managed to keep her secrets till the day she died, despite having ample time to speak to me while I nursed her at home every day of her last six months. What was the hold on her heart and her mind that made her lock her story away so securely? As I cooked for her and talked with her, as my baby played at the foot of her bed, as I washed her and tended to her body, fed her, medicated her, didn't she ever want to say: Sit down here, my darling. I have something to tell you.

But then, there are ways and ways of telling.

Mama's favourite film actor was Ingrid Bergman. The mysterious Swedish beauty was a star of her generation, and

Mama looked a bit like her. I imagine now that her lovers may have compared her to the enchanting lead in 1940s movies such as *Casablanca*, *Notorious* and *Joan of Arc*.

In the 1950s Bergman ruffled feathers when, already married, she not only had an affair with the Italian director Roberto Rossellini but had a son with him. She divorced her first husband (a Swedish dentist turned neurosurgeon who stalled the divorce, thereby making Bergman give birth to a bastard child); married Rossellini, had twin daughters, and in 1957 divorced him; then married the scion of a wealthy Swedish shipping family. All this made her persona non grata in Hollywood, but of great interest to Mama.

I fancy Mama thought that she and Ingrid Bergman would hit it off if they ever had a chance meeting. But that wasn't on the cards. I always knew that Bergman had an unconventional personal life, because Mama had alerted me to it. It meant little to me at the time, but now I was beginning to understand why she may have been trying to get me thinking.

I was enjoying reading about the life of Bergman and discovering that she really was thought of as evil, a corrupter of American womanhood. She was in a position to carry it off but a woman like Mama, a survivor, poor, uneducated and in a lowly position in a foreign country, might well have thought twice about blatantly doing the same thing.

It was distracting fun to watch Bergman in interviews on YouTube, to imagine what Mama saw in her. It took me away from the sadness of the Holocaust testimonies in the Shoah Archive—but I knew I had to get back to watching them, in order to further my quest.

I had discovered Vladka Meed. She survived the war by posing as a Catholic outside the walls of the Warsaw ghetto. Older than Mama, Meed was in a good position to move between the ghetto and the occupied city, as she later wrote in her memoir of the time, *On Both Sides of the Wall*.

She described how looking more like a Polish Catholic child than a Jewish one had always given her a feeling of security, as had the ability to speak Polish fluently and mingle with her neighbours. By the time the ghetto was established in Warsaw, in 1940, Meed was taking risks, sneaking through holes in the wall with stockings and other merchandise from her parents' former business, to trade on the outside for food and other necessities. Later, as a member of the Jewish underground, she smuggled a map of Treblinka out of the ghetto and sticks of gelignite back in on the return journey.

She watched the Warsaw ghetto uprising in 1943 from the outside. Mama told me once that she tried to enter the ghetto when she heard that the Jews were fighting back, because she was tired of living under the strain of her false identity and wanted to die. But the soldiers guarding the gates turned her away, saying it wasn't for people like her, just for Jews.

Here is Vladka Meed's memory of that night:

> At night I saw the flames of the ghetto. And I saw
> also certain pictures which were seared in my mind.
> Some Jews running from one place to the other
> and also seeing Jews jumping from buildings, but

I was observing this from a window and I couldn't do
anything. And then the flames burst into the ghetto.
The Germans couldn't take over the streets, they start
putting block after block on fire. They start burning
the ghettos...the buildings, and this was the uprising
which we...the small group on the Aryan side, we tried
to get through. We tried to communicate. We decided
even to go into the ghetto to be with them but it was,
everything was in vain. We didn't have any communication. We saw only tanks coming in, tanks going out,
or some ambulances going in and we're listening to
the shooting...we have to let the outside know what
is going on.

It was unnerving to read an account of the same moment
that had been related to me by Mama long ago. But, more
than that, Meed revealed the behaviours and attitudes that
she and Mama and all those with false identities had to culti-
vate for their survival.

Vladka Meed said she had to be careful that her eyes
didn't betray her identity. Jews trying to pass as non-Jews
often revealed themselves unwittingly by the sadness in
their eyes, she said, by seeing things that other Poles had
long since ceased to notice. She taught herself to give a deep,
joyous belly laugh which suggested a freedom and noncha-
lance that no Jew could possibly possess.

Meed would size up a situation quickly. She could get
people to talk about themselves and could quickly establish
rapport, revealing little of herself but absorbing essential
information from others. She was strong and resolute. She
was persistent, even stubborn.

Work by the Polish sociologist Małgorzata Melchior on other survivors in the same situation reveals that concealing their identity required people to suppress their fear, despair and doubts. As a result, some survivors suffered depression and other psychological disorders for years after the war ended.

'At the heart of the experience of the Jews who survived owing to false documents,' Melchior writes, 'was the strategy of camouflage, mimicry and dissolution in their social environment, so as not to be recognised as a Jew. Uncertainty, loneliness, fear and continuous lying—these were the elements of the adopted survival method and its inevitable costs.'

Camouflage; mimicry; refraining from showing fear, despair and doubts; and continuous lying. This is what Mama learned to do. So it is probably no surprise that she was capable of masking the fact of her children having different fathers. How easy must that have been, after living for three years with the constant threat of exposure in one of the deadliest places in the world.

In my first year of high school, when I got into trouble for passing notes to other students in geography, Mama was called in to speak to the headmaster. I was worried for her. She hadn't been to high school herself and I thought she would feel out of place. Her English was accented, her clothes were modest, and she might be confused about what the rules were and how I had contravened them.

I knew she had an appointment before recess, and when the bell rang I was full of dread.

I saw her across the yard, and she winked at me and

smiled. She had brazened her way through the meeting, noting that she was the only mother called to the school when several other kids had also been in on the plot. She asked if it was because we were Jewish. The headmaster buckled under the strain.

I was impressed. I had no idea then that this was the least of her accomplishments.

The historian Nechama Tec also survived in Warsaw. She said in video testimony that in a big city you could get lost in the crowd: there was less chance of being recognised by someone who'd lived in a town where your family was known. She too remarked on Jews being known for the sadness in their eyes. 'Warsaw became a hunting ground for Jews; many people had a business out of finding them and providing them to the Germans,' she said. 'After many of the ghettos of Poland were liquidated, people had the same idea as us [about pretending not to be Jewish].' She didn't talk about her experiences for thirty years.

My quest had started with a hunt for a mysterious father but it had morphed into a hunt for a mysterious mother, too. It took Nechama Tec three decades to talk, but after three decades Mama was busy dying. She was unable to speak to us about that, either. From what I saw in the Tec interview, there were ways of being that were important to maintaining a false identity. How could I write about my identity without investigating a mother whose own identity was tied up in questions of survival?

For her book *Resilience and Courage*, Tec interviewed the concentration-camp survivor Karla Szajewicz-Frist, who compared her lot to those like Mama on the Aryan side.

We were fatalists; we were all together; those who were on the Aryan side didn't have anyone to lean on; they were constantly on guard, constantly afraid they'd be discovered. All the time a person had to think, How do I walk? How do I look? What do they think? And so on. One was always tense. But we in the camp, we became robots...I got some comfort from thinking that I was in the same boat as everyone else.

Tec also spoke to those who, like her, got by on the outside under a false identity. Dvora Rosenbaum-Fogel, a Hungarian survivor, said: 'When they arrested us...I was glad. Why? Because to be in hiding, your heart beats fast all the time. You are always scared.'

Zwia Rechtman-Schwartz said: 'From the moment I parted from my mother, I was very much alone until the end of the war. I did not trust anybody; I did not talk to anybody; I was not ready to open up for anybody. I had a wall inside me.'

Leah Silverstein said:

With nobody to console you, with nobody to tell you it's okay, it will be better, hold on, then you are in total isolation. Total loneliness. You know you are among people, and you are like an island. You have to make life-threatening decisions all by yourself...It is like playing Russian roulette with your life...Day after day.

These survivors spoke about the pressure of having to lie all the time and of the wish to 'be oneself', to tell someone who they were, to inform their families about what had happened to them should they die; even to be found out and therefore able to stop pretending, though it might mean death. This surely was Mama's mental state when she tried to get into the Warsaw ghetto, and was turned away.

She once told me that she'd forgotten how to speak Yiddish by the time the war ended, such was the repression she'd endured in order not to give herself away. She said she was worried that she might shout out Yiddish words in her dreams when, at one point, she was sharing a room with two other women.

I thought of Mama's silence over the identity of my father, and of her adherence—albeit inconsistently—to the Orthodox habits of her childhood in the *shtetl*. Why, I thought again, would such an expert evader tell a truth so profound, so destructive?

A poem came to mind, by my favourite poet, the Polish Nobel Prize winner Wisława Szymborska. 'Autotomy' describes the way a sea cucumber divides itself in two when it senses danger. One part is offered to its fate and, with the other, an escape is made: 'To die as much as necessary, without going too far. / To grow back as much as needed, from the remnant that survives.'

18

Stranger on a train

SOME days as I sat alone listening to people's horrific recollections in a variety of languages, which required a lot of concentration, I worried that I was getting too swept up in the multitude of stories instead of following the ones I had set out to find. When I read Gunnar S. Paulsson's *Secret City: The Hidden Jews of Warsaw, 1940–1945* I could feel myself breathing shallowly and it seemed to be more than just the bronchitis I'd contracted that winter, which was hard to shake. I thought I might have been breathing like that because I was casting myself back to Mama's early life, trying to be her, toughing it out brazenly while terrified of being unmasked.

I have a photo of her taken after the war in which she is looking over one shoulder and laughing. How could she laugh? I was always puzzled by this. She knew by then that all of her family had been killed; she was an orphan, a stateless minor with no money and no education. Now I see the laugh as her disguise. This was how she evaded the interest of the Gestapo. She looked like she couldn't possibly be a Jewish girl hiding her identity. I remembered Vladka

Meed's comment about learning to give a deep and joyous belly laugh.

Looking at the photo reminded me of a meeting with the writer Hanna Krall on that trip to Poland in the 1990s. I was introduced through a Polish cultural attaché to Krall, who met me for lunch at the Hotel Europejski in Warsaw, from the outset seeming reluctant and mysterious. Her area of interest was Polish–Jewish–German relations and she might have been tired of being wheeled out by the cultural bureaucrats, or maybe she was just tired. She had survived the war as a child, her Jewish origins hidden by a series of Polish families. After the war she was placed in an orphanage.

Krall was now in her sixties, direct and charming but vulnerable and sharp as glass, and just as ready to wound. She was as I imagined Mama might have been at that age, had she lived.

She'd brought me an English translation of one of her books to read. 'I will never come to Australia,' she said. 'It is too far.'

But, I said, there are many people who would love to hear you and to read your books.

'They will survive without me,' she said, with finality.

We talked about her work, which she said was like my trip to the villages and the towns in the backblocks. She did this all the time, she explained—went to places where Jews used to live and asked questions.

Then she said: 'I decided today on the way to the hotel to end my marriage of thirty-seven years and leave my husband.'

'Today? On the way? Do you have another man?'

'No,' she said. 'But my organism tells me it's enough.'

This sat between us like a cloud. I didn't know what I was supposed to say. I thought of the word 'supposed', because it felt like Krall's alarming conversational gambit invited me to follow a script.

'Why today?'

'See,' she said, 'I am telling all these interesting stories about Jews and what happened to me, and all you can think about is if I will leave my husband today.'

She'd been told that I was a serious Australian journalist. 'I don't like serious journalism,' she said.

We talked about her lonely childhood before her mother gave her up to the first Polish family, and afterwards. She came to a story about a time when she and her mother were stopped in the street by a Polish policeman. Her mother was blond and blue-eyed (a 'good look'—that's what everyone still called the combination), yet Krall was dark-haired and brown-eyed.

The policeman asked Krall's mother to recite a well-known Catholic prayer, and she faltered; then he asked Hanna, aged seven, who repeated it perfectly.

'I don't know what to do,' he said. 'A woman who doesn't look Jewish but doesn't know the prayer, and a child who looks Jewish but does know it. Who is the Jew here and who is the Pole? You decide between you and I'll come and take the Jew in the morning.'

Hanna said that she and her mother, who was then thirty-seven, talked all night. Her mother said she'd already lived her life and Hanna should be the Pole. Hanna said she was too young to survive on her own, and that her grand-mother and uncles and others depended on her mother, too.

Finally they arrived at a solution. They would both be Jews and they would both die. They were happy with the decision.

When the policeman came, the Polish family they were living with covered for them and talked him out of thinking that either one of them was Jewish. Hanna said that she thought it was Mary, mother of Jesus, who saved them, as when she had recited the prayer in the street in front of the policeman she had really meant it.

There in the Hotel Europejski foyer she started to falter and then to weep, and couldn't go on. I reached out to hold her hand and she removed it. I must have looked alarmed.

She saw this and made a gesture with her eyes, opening them wider and staring at me with frozen rage, as if to say: What are you looking at me like that for? She reminded me of Mama with her aggressive sadness, and I started to weep, too.

We both blew our noses on paper serviettes and she said: 'Quickly, ask me about my husband again. Ask me if I've decided to leave him for good. Then we won't cry.'

We laughed. Then we talked some more.

And later, when I was walking her out of the hotel, she said, 'Well, what do you think, shall I leave my husband?'

'I'm not going to give you advice,' I said. 'You're old enough to make up your own mind.'

I asked again if there really wasn't anyone else.

She told me about a doctor who practised near her *dacha* in the country and was very handsome. He attended her for some trouble with her leg. He put a drain tube into it and needed to check on her day after day. Then the tube disappeared into her leg and she went to see him, full of alarm.

'What a pity it wasn't a needle,' he said. 'I'm great at getting needles out, I was for years in Africa doing this.'

She said she got angry with him, and realised that he'd never read any of her books and that she couldn't tolerate a man like this, who probably would never read them.

Did her husband read her works?

'Oh yes,' she said. 'He's a very intelligent, learned man.'

As she left she said: 'Write to me about what you think of my work. But don't write, "Have you left your husband yet?" I'm talking to you because you are like a stranger on a train.'

I know, I said, exactly like a stranger on a train.

I did read her book of two distinct parts, *The Subtenant* and *To Outwit God*. *The Subtenant* is a strange and complex autobiographical novella in which the narrator has an imagined conversation over forty years with the child who survived the war in the apartment of the narrator's Polish family.

The child was sometimes taken for a walk by her Polish protectors, but she had dark Jewish eyes, so the mother of the household had her walk with her eyes downcast so that no one would look into them. She suggested that the child kick a stone as she walked, to keep her eyes looking down and avoid suspicion. Later her lowered eyes are likened to those of Pliny's wild beast Catoblepas, who kept them lowered as his head was so heavy—which was fortunate, because anyone who looked into them died.

'Do you see the striking analogy?' the narrator says. 'The eyes of Catoblepas killed others, yours could kill you.'

Was that a death stare that Hanna Krall had given me in the foyer of the Hotel Europejski?

And now that I look at the book again I see her inscription: *For Ramona, with whom we talk about the same world, with whom we cry...*Her name, and then: *Warsaw, 10/7/1996.* It looked as though I had cut through the sharpness of her personality—at the least she was recognising the moment that we cried together.

After I returned home from that trip I sent Krall a handwritten note, telling her that I'd read her book and that her story reminded me of my mother's. And that she was like my mother in many respects. She never replied.

Some of Mama's behaviours must have come from her experience of growing up alone. I felt watched over and restricted by her when I was a teenager. But it was different when I was younger. On my first day at a new school after we'd moved suburbs, she walked me there. I was in Grade One. Before we left, she told me to watch how we got there (up our street, across the big road at the lights, down the next street, across the small road), but I was so thrilled and happy and scared to be going to a new school that I didn't take it in. Leaving me at school, she said that she'd wait at home for me and I could get back myself. *Because I have shown you what to do.* I nodded and kissed her goodbye.

It was a big day of play lunch and lunch and afternoon playtime and new people and a new room and a new desk and a new teacher, so by home time I was muddled. I didn't reverse the order of the morning's walk and thought that there was a big road first. I looked up and down for a place to cross with lights but I couldn't find it. Eventually I went back to the school, and all the kids were gone and the mothers, too. I wandered into our classroom block and found the headmistress in her office. She asked where my mother was and I told her I was supposed to find my own way home. She looked up her records and put me in her car.

At the front door I could tell she was angry with Mama. I had the impression that the headmistress regarded her as a bad mother, and looked down on her accent. She explained that I was too young to be expected to find my way home on the first day.

I remember my mother's almost haughty expression. I imagine she was thinking that this headmistress had no idea of what was possible in the world, what was dangerous, what was a risk.

Now I suspect that, perhaps unconsciously, Mama was trying to future-proof me, preparing me for a time when I might have to survive on my own. Expecting a five-year-old to navigate backwards a simple ten-minute walk from home to school? Other five-year-old children she'd seen had to survive a war zone, hunger, cold, loneliness and the predations of strangers.

My sister's husband tells an anecdote about his mother, who'd been in a concentration camp, putting him on a bus to kindergarten. He had no idea how to get off, where to get off or what to do when he got there. These stories are not cause for pity, but rather a means for us to try to understand the mindset of survivors.

I turned six later that year and had settled in at the new school when Mama told me that the children who went to school with her—the Polish kids in that tiny village in the countryside, at the intersection of two dirt roads—gave her away when the Germans marched in and asked for the Jews to stand up. She moved into the ghetto with all the others.

I wonder why she told me that story then. It was a new school: did she want to give me the rundown on all the possibilities? Surely this wasn't a story to make me feel confident. Had I asked her what the new school would be like, what her school was like in Poland? She must have said something about her survival method and her change of identity to me, or maybe I overheard it.

At school, when the teacher asked us to put up our hands if we were Jewish, I knew what I had to do. My right hand stayed firmly under the desk, clamped there by the left one.

I watched as two or three other children stuck their hands into the air. They were asked to stand and come to the front of the class. This was it, I thought. And, because I was the new girl, I didn't know any of them and couldn't warn them. So I sat very still. They filed out of the room.

A nice woman came into the class to teach us for one lesson a week. She was a religious-instruction volunteer from the local Presbyterian Church.

I learned the Lord's Prayer. *Our father who art in heaven, please don't let them find out I'm Jewish.* I was good at remembering the stories and the songs, and my hand shot up when the woman asked us a question. I was a model Christian. I felt a pang of regret as the other Jewish kids filed out each week for a session with the rabbi, but it was too late to own up.

I liked the tales about Jesus, especially the miracles. I was impressed with the loaves and fishes, and the walking on water. No wonder that when it came to choosing a responsible child to be Mary, they looked no further than me.

I came home one day in early December and asked Mama if I could take a tea towel to school.

'Are you going to cook something, Ramona?'

'No, it's for a play.'

'What kind of a play?'

'It's just a play about a lady with a baby and she wears a tea towel around her head. It's nothing, really.'

'So what does this lady with the baby and the tea towel on her head actually do?'

'She just sits in a chair, in a zoo.'

'You mean there are animals with this baby?'

'A few.'

'Would this be a Christmas play, by any chance?'

'Yeah, maybe that's what it is.'

'Do they know you are Jewish, Ramona?'

Why was I surprised that you knew so much about nativity plays, Mama?

I told her about the safety aspects of religious-instruction classes and that, as she had survived by pretending to be Christian, I'd thought that learning to be one was a good idea.

She took me to school the next morning, to the headmaster's office, and blew my cover. He was aghast. Where were they going to find a replacement Mary at this late stage? They didn't have an understudy.

'Don't forget, sir, that Mary was one of us!' Mama said.

The headmaster was relieved.

And on the morning of the play, the local reverend patted my head as I walked by him with the tea towel on and the doll in my arms, and Mama stood in the audience with a distant look on her face, and I suspect that only I could see the tears in her eyes.

Despite the mysteries and confusions, I knew my mother loved me. She let my sister and me come into her bed in the mornings, and held us while we cuddled her and fought for our territory, which was marked by an imaginary line between her breasts and down her body. She told us that education was important. She let us do our homework without making us do too much around the house. She thought we should have ballet lessons and piano lessons. She started to teach me how to cook only when she realised she was dying.

She'd been tired for a long time, and for a while she went to her GP and then to skin specialists about a rash. At her annual check-up her gynaecologist, the doctor who had delivered my sister and me, suggested she have a blood test.

When she went back for the result—and I am only guessing here—the doctor told her that she had chronic myeloid leukaemia and that it was fatal. I wonder what she said. I wonder why she asked the doctor to ring me.

But there I was, in my second year of university, at nineteen, home with my sister, who was fifteen, and a telephone call in the afternoon from the doctor announces that my mother is very sick, she has leukaemia, she is going to die and she is coming home now on the tram. And I am not to tell my little sister about it.

Feeling numb, I placed the phone in its cradle. The afternoon sun shone into the lounge room, turning everything a sickly gold. After a while I heard Mama climbing the steps. She came in and asked if the doctor had called me, and said she was going to start taking some pills. I read the label on the bottle but it held no meaning for me. She began making dinner. She didn't talk about what the prognosis was, about how long she thought she was going to live, or what would happen to us when she died. She had her closed face on, eyes deep and blue and giving nothing way. I knew better than to ask anything.

In the following days she began to retreat under her blanket on the couch, reading and dozing. I went to university; my sister went to school. I learned the lessons she had to teach me: to show nothing on my face, not to cry, not to ask questions, not to cause my sister any anxiety, not to make waves.

We listened to Charles Aznavour, whose chansons she liked. She told me she'd heard a song on the radio that she wanted me to buy for her. She said it was called 'Time in a Bottle'. I found out that it was by Jim Croce, and when I brought it home she would listen to it over and over.

We didn't talk about that either. We didn't really have to. The song's lyrics were her way of saying that she was sad to be leaving us. But she couldn't find it in herself to tell us directly. Her disguise lasted all the way, through more than thirty years from the war's end, to the moment she took her last breath.

19

A citizen of the earth

MY sister saw an announcement in the paper that Dad's wife had died. I was surprised not to have heard already, as I would have liked to have gone to her funeral, to pay my respects. I rang her daughter and left a message, but she never returned the call.

Some months later I noticed her as I stood in the queue at Target. She seemed to be crouching behind a dress rack. Was she trying to avoid me? I sought her out and expressed my sympathies for her mother's death. She mumbled a little, and I said I would've liked to go to the funeral but no one had told my sister or me about it. She mumbled again and said she wasn't yet able to talk about her mother. She was upset and weirdly evasive. Weirdly? Maybe I had become so used to my mother being dead—it had been nearly four decades by this time—that I didn't regard the loss of a parent as tragic when the parent was old.

Dad's wife had inherited his estate and had then, I assumed, left everything to her daughter. It happens all the time, of course. I never thought I had any rights to him as my father, or any claim on his belongings.

I looked up the details of her death online. She was eighty-five when she died and had been cremated at a different cemetery to the one where Dad's grave is. Long ago, he had bought a plot for himself at the Orthodox Jewish cemetery next to one for a card-playing friend of his. He couldn't buy one for her, as she wasn't Jewish. It was an odd thing for him to do, but it was not the first odd thing.

So I was surprised to see on the burial record that her religion was stated as Jewish. She was cremated, which is not allowed in Jewish Orthodoxy, and her ashes were at the necropolis next door to the Orthodox cemetery. I saw that she was a couple of years older than Mama would have been, had Mama lived beyond forty-nine. She had died on 9 March and been cremated three days later. You're supposed to be buried quickly, and three days is unusual, unless the body needs to be repatriated or close relatives have to fly in from overseas. If she was properly converted, why wasn't she buried near Dad?

Then I saw that Temple Beth Israel, the liberal Jewish congregation which held the Sunday school classes I had attended, had a notice of her death. Why was I picking over the ashes of this woman who'd looked after Dad until his awful death? Why was I questioning her right to be interred in the way that she and her family saw fit?

I found the records for Mama and Dad. As in life, when they could hardly stand to be in the same room together, in death they were far removed, too. Her 1977 death placed her in Row 3, plot B8, while his 2008 death had him in Row 20, plot D12. But he was more removed by distance from his second wife. Her ashes are interred a way down the road.

I looked up the records for Max. He'd died on 13 January 1989. He was buried somewhere between Mama and Dad, Row 18, grave S5. Was the placement fitting? He hardly needed to come between them in death, as so much else came between them in life.

I remembered the first phone call from Bern after she'd met Max at the auction and he'd asked after me, asked if I was happy. It was in my first years of full-time broadcasting, which started in 1988. He may well have known by then that he was dying. He might have been thinking about his life and putting some things to rest. But then, why would he have been at an auction? Maybe he was always going to auctions; maybe they were a hobby for him.

Like Dad, Max didn't leave me anything. I was tempted to get sentimental about him, but he had plenty of chances to contact me after that day he'd been reminded of me by seeing Bern. And if she hadn't been looking for a house, they would never have met and he would never have asked about me.

I checked on Max's brother Joe, the one who couldn't be told about my existence because of the shame. He'd died, too. His younger son had told me that Max and his father often fought about their business. Joe was the tailor and Max was the businessman; Max wasn't a fine tailor like Joe. Of course Max was the businessman, I thought. He had learned everything about how to do business, how to *organise*, in his years at Auschwitz.

One night the following year I was watching a television documentary about the caves under Easter Island when the phone rang. It was Joe's younger son's wife. She told me that

Alan had died, aged sixty-three. He'd had pneumonia, after serious lung disease, and had continued smoking. He'd still ridden his horse each day around Kuranda, and someone at his funeral recalled him wearing a Zorro costume. His kids were now young teenagers. His mother was still alive: eighty-eight years old and in a retirement home.

He'd been in Melbourne with his daughter some months before his death and hadn't called or visited me. I wasn't surprised, but I felt left out. He was possibly my half-brother, and I only met him that one time. He'd died some weeks ago. His poor mother, outliving her only child.

Meanwhile, I'd got in touch with Mr Lederman's adoptive son to tell him I had written about his father, and ask what he knew about his parents' marriage and their history together. He knew very little. When he was growing up he didn't think it polite to probe too much. He said that Mr Lederman had indeed been a truck driver in the Red Army, but had defected during the war because he didn't like the way the Soviets treated their underlings. Along with three others he deserted, taking the army truck and ending up behind German enemy lines. After the German defeat the Soviets found them, and his three companions were executed on the spot. Mr Lederman was set free, as his captors couldn't believe a Jew would drive towards Nazi Germany during the war unless he'd made a dreadful mistake. Hearing this, I thought Mr Lederman might have been a bit dim for the likes of Mama. I still had not forgiven him for his cowardice towards us.

What was I left with as each of the players in my drama slowly faded off stage? That old Yiddish joke about the man who's proud of his antecedents being like a potato: the best part of him is underground.

The 1894 translation of *The Memoirs of Jacques Casanova de Seingalt* (the name under which the adventurer, intellectual and lover Giacomo Casanova wrote) starts with 'My Family Pedigree', which the author can cite from the elopement of his relative Don Jacob Casanova, the illegitimate son of Don Francisco Casanova, a native of Saragosa, the capital of Aragon: 'in the year of 1428 he carried off Dona Anna Palofax from her convent, on the day after she had taken the veil.' He charts seven generations of his father's family and, from his mother's side, the story of her romance with and marriage to his father, until his own birth on 2 April 1725.

In light of Casanova's reputation as a daring lover, the first story of the flight from the convent of the bastard with the newly minted nun is but a precursor to many of the adventures of the author himself. You soon forget about the stories that went before, as Casanova tells his own recollections and adventures so well. Apart from the family tree being a useful literary device, what does it matter to me how he arrived on the planet?

After his mother died, my husband showed me some photographs of his mother's family sent to him by his first cousin. There was his grandfather and his great-grandmother. He looked to see if there was a resemblance; he saw a similar nose. And then he filed the pictures away.

I asked what he saw when he looked at these people. He said that he remembered some of them. There wasn't much connection there, it seemed to me. His family ties were much looser than mine.

If I had pictures going back three or four generations, I thought, I would be entranced. But how long would that last? How entranced would I be if there was no loss to deal with, no tragedies?

I'd been looking at images of pre-World War II Polish Jews on a memorial website. They were affecting photos, because they were taken at all kinds of family events: birthdays, weddings, dinners. One showed a girl of about eleven leaning into a large chair on which sat her cousins, girl twins, all of them dressed in their best clothes. I shudder to think what happened to them. They are connected to me in ways that are sociological and cultural, although not familial. Would my shuddering be more profound if we shared blood ties?

In an interview the great Australian writer Elizabeth Harrower told me that, while she'd never had children, she thought of us as all belonging to the same family. There were very few human beings once, and now we are numerous but connected. Why should we want our 'own' families ahead of others?

When I first read Dovid Hofshteyn's poem I thought it was melancholy. *We spring from rocks / from rocks ground by millstones of time*...Not knowing where I sprang from, I had only barren rocks with which to make a claim for my history.

Now I think of it as a poem for all life, not just for the human species. We did all spring from rocks: geological time threw up the right conditions for our species to hold sway on the planet. It wasn't always so, and it won't always be.

Where do I come from? Why must we ask this question?

Does coming from somewhere tell us anything about where we are and who we are? Does coming from somewhere give us more than the right to claim land, or a history, or a culture?

I know without doubt that I come from the remnant Jewish population of Poland gathered together after World War II and flung to this far region of the planet. I am from the Yiddish-speaking, Orthodox-practising population of the *shtetls*.

I know I am descended from a rural family near the town of Sokołów Podlaski, because my maternity is not in doubt. My access to the family stories from this branch is limited by the early death of my mother, and by her lack of inclination when alive to tell many of them. This is understandable, as she was a child survivor of the Holocaust and the only surviving member of her family. She was traumatised by her history. And I was too young to formulate a set of questions that I could ask her. So there is a significant historical gap in my knowledge.

But say I could know as much as I wanted to know: what would it mean? What does it mean to people who can trace their roots back? How much does it connect you to a person you may have directly descended from? Would it matter for four generations? Five? And then what?

I spent a weekend in the home of a friend who has pictures of her English relatives, many generations back, fixed to the wall in the hall. There are women in long crinolines, preparing for a ball or sitting next to their respectable husbands. I had a pang of longing when I saw them all set out like this.

I fantasised about having just such a set of pictures, reaching back through both the maternal and paternal lines. The bearded serious grandfathers, the Orthodox women with wigs on their heads. (Because of which, I might not be able to see if their hair was curly or reddish or black as coal.)

What traits do we get from these people? Beyond the shape of our faces or the colour of our hair, or the inheritance of money and property, what do they give us? Do they help in our understanding of the lives we lead and the choices that are available to us and the decisions we make?

My grandmother Rivka, from whom I got my Hebrew name—who, before she died in her thirties, decided in 1942 to send her only blond-haired, blue-eyed fourteen-year-old daughter away to an uncertain future, but one that was less certain to contain death than the one which she shared with her darker, brown-eyed son—made a wrenching decision that guaranteed my birth on a continent a world away. Does her story tell me anything about what I might be capable of?

And why then does it matter to me who my father was? If I knew, would I be any clearer about the contribution of his parents or their parents to the person I am, or the life that I have lived or the future stories of my grandchildren?

Why does the story of the Khazar Jews make me want to search online for a portrait of their likeness? What might a picture of a Khazar Jewish princess with curly reddish hair and blue eyes and a face shaped like mine tell me? Given the length of time involved, the chances that I'd look like my fanciful Khazar princess are probably small.

When I look at my own grandchildrens' faces, I see how the contributions of their fathers' families change the shapes of their eyes from mine—or my chin, or my hair. My eldest granddaughter has the almond-shaped eyes of her Filipino-Spanish mezisto grandfather, my blue eyes and curls, and elements I imagine her father may have inherited from his Indigenous Australian great-grandmother. She is just as close to me as if she were my perfect clone, and the differences that make her who she is delight me.

One day, my husband used computer software to see what the possibilities were when Max's and Mama's faces were combined. We had to find original photos of our subjects facing in the same direction, so it was a bit restricted, but I was convinced that my face was an approximation of theirs. It was a little spooky. I played with the software for a while, changing the percentages—less Max, more Mama; more Max, less Mama—and then I put it aside, just like my husband had done with his family photos.

They said it would take three months to arrive, but I was anxious when that time had almost elapsed and my Polish passport had not come. For most of the third month I checked the letterbox each day for special deliveries. I searched my calendar to see exactly when I had handed over my papers at the consulate in Sydney. It was Tuesday, 30 July 2013, and on Wednesday, 30 October 2013, three months to the day, a man from Australia Post brought the registered letter from the Consulate General of the Republic of Poland to my door.

I could even read some of the writing in it, as I had engaged a Polish teacher to give me weekly lessons. Learning Polish had ceased to be full of anxiety and had turned into a pleasurable interest for me. I thought I would never master the complex grammar, but I was learning words and phrases and was even able to decode signs in the historical footage I found on YouTube. I enthusiastically attended Polish film screenings and could understand some of the dialogue without reading the English subtitles. I was especially taken by films set in the pre-war period and post-war Soviet times, and shot in black-and-white. I was under the illusion that they brought me closer to my quarry.

My EU passport was finally before me, all present and correct and above board. I was now a legitimate citizen of the Republic of Poland. But, I reminded myself, I was already a legitimate citizen of the Commonwealth of Australia before all this started.

Over the course of this winding journey I had at least learned that I am determined. I am like a dog searching for a bone, a bloodhound, even if I am still not sure of where all my blood comes from.

With my two passports I am now a citizen of the earth. Although the past is important, the future is what excites me, and my passport to it requires me to take one breath, one step and one day at a time. One step, one day at a time. It sounds like a program for alcoholics. Was I unhealthily addicted to the story of where I came from?

I saw Wagner's Ring Cycle and realised that I was not alone. There are great traditions, across cultures and time, of asking the same questions: Who is the father? Who is the mother? This importance of tracing the godly lines, the questions of inheritance, the confusions between princes and paupers, the ways in which human beings try to avoid their fates by taking on other identities, the wandering gods in disguise, the myths and legends: they all point to the importance of our identity. Many of Shakespeare's plays have a disguised or mistaken identity at their heart.

I understand now that I was missing not just a collection of family photographs and a family tree showing blood ties, but the stories upon stories that they might have told and I would have loved to hear. Of how their families found their ways to this part of Poland and in which year, after which pogrom or family tragedy. Maybe one of them went off and became something unexpected—a court advisor or a famous soldier or a courtesan or a thief or a slave.

We need our stories: they are the way we learn about the world, and the way we pass on what we learn to those who come after us. We are always looking for a plausible story, one that might fit the meagre facts, as they do in courts of law—never really able to know the whole truth but finding the most likely explanation, the most convincing thread.

How do I imagine Mama's story went?

She knew by the time they'd left Poland and spent four years in Paris, in that fourth-floor room with the treadle sewing machines and the piecework that they did late into the nights, that he was not the man for her. He cried too much. She had lost everyone, too, but she had learned not to cry. He was nearly ten years older than her, yet such a baby. She didn't want to leave the City of Light. She had nothing much there—but it was Paris, after all.

Her second cousin who'd survived with his parents in Siberia came to Paris and convinced her that if she made the boat trip across the world to Australia, where he had a distant relative from another branch of his family, he would help her to leave her miserable marriage.

That promise came to nothing once they were all in Melbourne. Another factory. Another slum. What was the point? What was a poor, uneducated survivor of barely twenty-three years of age to do on her own in this god-forsaken faraway city? She could hardly speak English, much less get a job that might support a woman on her own. It was 1950. Women didn't do that.

And her husband blamed her for his misery. If only I had a child, he said, I would be a father and I would have something to live for. She had seen doctors in Paris and she began seeing another one, a woman, in the new city. They found nothing wrong with her. And him? They didn't broach that subject. It had been eight years and still she couldn't get pregnant. It was a monthly reason for an argument.

She read books. She had dreams. She watched films. In the block of flats where she and Dad lived, some neighbours had a son who was an actor, and they offered a hand of friendship. They felt sorry for her, a survivor from the ashes of Nazi Europe, and invited her to go to the theatre with them.

She worked in a series of factory jobs. Her friend Isabel told her of a position as a finisher in a factory where she worked. It was run by two brothers. The older one had come to Melbourne before the war and established himself. The younger one survived Auschwitz and came to Australia to join him. Mama went to the factory and started working there.

The younger brother was handsome and tall and strong. He was married; he had a young son. When he seemed to be interested in her, she went along with it. Why not? Who cared what happened to her? Nobody, least of all her. She went with him to the room with the low bed and the single bare light. It wasn't romantic, but it was urgent and passionate.

She returned to her chair in the machinists' section. She saw him walk to his office between the women bent low over their work, and she wondered if any others had been taken into the little room. She felt something like hope, like excitement. He was older even than her husband, old enough to protect her.

When she went for the appointment with her doctor she could hardly believe what she was hearing. At last! She didn't call her husband. She didn't call the boss. She went for a walk through the gardens between the doctor's office and the city, and later found herself in a movie theatre. The film was *Roman Holiday*, with Audrey Hepburn playing a visiting European princess who escapes her guardians to explore Rome for a day on her own. She meets Gregory Peck, an American reporter, older, who shelters her.

It's the story of a disguise, the princess pretending to be someone other than who she is. Just for a day. Mama was familiar with this kind of story, and she must have preferred the short and romantic one to the long and brutal one she had lived.

Maybe she told Max that she was carrying his child. Maybe, as Isabel said, she loved him. Maybe he loved her, too, and left his wife and son in the hope that they could be together. But he went back to his family. Maybe Max's wife found out he was having an affair and threw him out. Maybe it was just till she had cooled down. Maybe he never intended to come to Mama.

She never went back to work at the factory. Dad was pleased: his wife was pregnant and he was going to be a father at last. Mama was a practical woman. She might have thought that living with Dad was better than the life Max could have offered. If he offered anything at all.

Her life in disguise would go on.

She resisted having another child for years, until my pleading for a sister or brother got to her. She made her arrangements again. The children would never know: no one would ever know for sure. Her secret was hinted at in her occasional comments; perhaps she sometimes wanted to tell everything, or her unconscious mind allowed the comments to bubble to the surface, only for her to close the lid smartly, under the resolute gaze of her older daughter.

I was complicit, going along with her habit of silence and privacy. And finally her secret followed her to her grave, hinted at only by the persistent collection of small pebbles that I would find on the rare occasions I visited it, telling me that someone had been to her resting place, and set down on the cold grey slab the customary sign, a gift of stones.

Robert Antelme's *The Human Race* reveals how stories were life-saving for the men in the slave-labour camps—a way to maintain their humanity, and to see the humanity in others. Antelme describes a Christmas Eve when one work detail was holed up in a church, their small bread portions eaten, and nothing more to come:

They talked about their wives and their kids. They were proper women, the wives, and they had their whims. The stories moved around the stove...They understood what each other was talking about, and they could go on like that for a long time. Everything was described: the metro line, the street leading to the house, the job, all sorts of jobs. The story didn't wear out easily, there was always something left to tell. The hell of memory was operating at full blast... at that point each one had become a figure in a story... then the party died down, the story petered out, nothing of it was left. What remained was the warmth upon our face, the stove's warmth, that had brought the stories forth.

The most eager to talk, those who talked the most, fell still...Somebody in the centre of the church started singing. He was trying to make the guys keep on forgetting their stomachs, to make them think of something else for a while. Nobody joined him, but he continued to sing by himself. Where was the singer? How could you recognise which one it had been? They were all lying down, buried under their blankets. All you heard was a vague murmur coming from the pallets. In each head were wife and bread and the street, all mixed up with the rest, with hunger, cold and filth.

Each a tiny source of warmth, these stories reminded Antelme and his fellow prisoners that they were still men, still human in the face of the inhuman treatment of them by their guards; the stories were evidence of their difference from other animals, their ability as human beings to use the complex grammar of their language to create a scene for themselves and for the others that would stir the emotions and engage the mind.

And here, in the warm stove of connection that I had made for myself, were the stories of Max and Mama and Dad and Mr Lederman and Isabel and Alan and the mad Queen of Songs and the unfinished marriage certificate and Hanna Krall with the death-ray eyes and Wanda Bujalska and the performers of Warsaw making counterfeit documents and the wild Khazar women on horseback meeting Levantine traders on the Silk Road and Moshe Wilner climbing the clock tower in Mława holding the town's time in his hands and the last days of Ötzi up in the icy reaches of the Austro-Italian border five thousand years ago: all these tales and so many others were now mine to tell. And the people I had doggedly followed had become characters in my story and I had become one in theirs, even though they would never know it.

I began my quest by asking: who am I? And I found the answer to a different question: what am I? I am made of stories.

We cherish our stories and, even if they have gaps, they continue to nourish us and to hold us secure as we make new ones, until we fade into the memories of others, mythic, dreamlike, forever silent. This is how it always is in the songlines of our lives: in the ending of one song are the seeds of a new one, the chorus we sing together, our melodies, coalescing into the greater human symphony.

Mama & Ramona, 1955.

Sources

BOOKS & JOURNALS

Antelme, Robert. *The Human Race*, trans. Jeffrey Haight & Annie Mahler, Marlboro Press / Northwestern University Press, 1998. (Originally published as *L'Espèce humaine*, © Éditions Gallimard, Paris, 1957.)

Casanova, Giacomo. *The Memoirs of Jacques Casanova de Seingalt*, trans. Arthur Machen, 1894.

Goldstein, David B. *Jacob's Legacy: A Genetic View of Jewish History*, Yale University Press, 2008.

Koestler, Arthur. *The Thirteenth Tribe*, Random House, 1976.

Krall, Hanna. *The Subtenant & To Outwit God*, trans. Jarosław Anders, Northwestern University Press, 1992.

Langbein, Hermann. *People in Auschwitz*, trans. Harry Zohn, University of North Carolina Press, 2004.

Levi, Primo. *The Drowned and the Saved*, trans. Raymond Rosenthal, Abacus, 1988.

Lichtenstein, Rachel, & Sinclair, Iain. *Rodinsky's Room*, Granta, 1999.

Meed, Vladka. *On Both Sides of the Wall: Memoirs from the Warsaw Ghetto*, trans. Steven Meed, Knopf Doubleday, 1979.

Oeggl, Klaus, et al. 'The reconstruction of the last itinerary of "Ötzi", the Neolithic Iceman, by pollen analyses from sequentially sampled gut extracts', *Quaternary Science Reviews*, 26: 7–8, 2007, pp. 853–61.

Ostrer, Harry. *Legacy: A Genetic History of the Jewish People*, Oxford University Press, 2012.

Paulsson, Gunnar S. *Secret City: The Hidden Jews of Warsaw, 1940–1945*, Yale University Press, 2002.

Richie, Alexandra. *Warsaw 1944: Hitler, Himmler, and the Warsaw Uprising*, Farrar, Straus and Giroux, 2013.

Sykes, Bryan. *The Seven Daughters of Eve: The Science that Reveals Our Genetic Ancestry*, W. W. Norton & Company, 2001.

Tec, Nechama. *Dry Tears: The Story of a Lost Childhood*, Oxford University Press, 1984.

Tec, Nechama. *Resilience and Courage: Women, Men, and the Holocaust*, Yale University Press, 2004.

Turnbull, David. 'Out of the glacier, into the freezer: Ötzi the "Iceman"—disruptive timings, spacings, and mobilities', in *Cryopolitics: Frozen Life in a Melting World*, ed. Joanna Radin & Emma Kowal (forthcoming).

Wasserstrom, Dunia. 'Testimony from the Auschwitz Trial, April 23, 1964', quoted in *Holocaust Historiography in Context: Emergence, Challenges, Polemics & Achievements*, ed. David Bankier & Dan Michman, Berghahn Books, 2008.

WEBSITES

Center for Holocaust & Genocide Studies, University of Minnesota: chgs.umn.edu

Genographic Project by National Geographic: genographic. nationalgeographic.com

Dovid Hofsteyn's 'We spring from rocks': mendele.commons. yale.edu/author/vbers/page/378

Cypora Jablon Zonszajn's Siedlce memoir: deathcamps.org/ occupation/siedlcememo.html

Nathaniel Kahn's *My Architect: A Son's Journey*: vimeo.com/9418890

Jane Korman's '...And now we dance: a celebration of life after Auschwitz': youtube.com/watch?v=CuvgUZeUo8Y

Małgorzata Melchior's 'The Holocaust survivors who passed as non-Jews in Nazi-occupied Poland and France': fondationshoah. org/fms/docpdf/coinchercheurs/melchior.pdf

Pinkas Hakehillot Polin's Mława chapter, *Encyclopedia of Jewish Communities in Poland*: jewishgen.org/yizkor/pinkas_poland/ pol4_00280.html

This American Life, 'The Ghost of Bobby Dunbar', 14 March 2008: thisamericanlife.org/radio-archives/episode/352/ the-ghost-of-bobby-dunbar

University of Southern California Shoah Foundation: sfi.usc.edu

Dr Izhak Ze'ev Yunis's 'The Old Hometown': zchor.org/ mlayunis.htm

Acknowledgments

My sincere thanks to Leszek Borkowski, Krystyna Duszniak, Monika Dzierba, Lena Fiszman and the Jewish Holocaust Museum and Research Centre, Helen Garner, Kerrie Haines, Marcia Jacobs, Lloyd Jones, Walter Lederman, Faith Liddell, Miriam Mahemoff, Iola Mathews and the Writers Victoria Glenfern studios, Agnieszka Morawiñska, Yoni Prior, the late Jacob Rosenberg, David Sornig, Slowko Tomyn, David Turnbull, and Michał Wiśniewski, all of whom helped in their own ways with my research for this book over many years.

As always, thanks to Text Publishing—especially Michael Heyward, David Winter, Jane Novak, and W. H. Chong.

I am immensely grateful to Bernadette Waldron, whose phone call all those years ago pointed me in a new and compelling direction.

And for their help, which was a testament to the kindness of strangers, I am indebted to Robin Dunne, Helen Dunne, Ray Dunne, the late Joseph Dunne, and the late Alan Dunne.

Finally, loving thanks to my husband, my daughters, my sons-in-law, my brother-in-law, and especially to my sister.

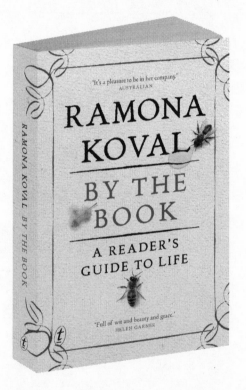